Dedicated to
My Husband
Aaron Smith

Special Thanks to
Aaron Moffo, Graphic Designer
Patty Lee & Rulena Smith, Proofreading

Table of Contents

Introduction
The Vision

Hi, my name is Kamra and I like apples. I always have. Nice, crunchy ones. Ones that spray juice onto your neighbor when you take a large bite out of it. I prefer them plain, room temperature and whole. But occasionally you may find me slicing them up and dipping them into peanut butter. I can eat a slice of apple pie if forced, down a cup of cider, and once in a blue moon have a cup of juice for breakfast. But nothing beats a plain apple plucked straight from a tree.

I grew up on a farm that had three simple apple trees in the backyard. Each summer my siblings and I would climb through the tight branches to the tops of the trees where the very best apples hung. There, they absorbed the most sunshine and rounded out like those on the bottom of the tree couldn't. The best ones were never in arms-reach, so to the very top we went! When the branches were at max capacity we'd get the tractor and be lifted in the bucket so we could gather from the tiptop. Shaking the branches with all our might, the apples would fall. This rain of fruit would bring an outburst of praise as we'd scurry to gobble them all up.

While a great deal of them were eaten right there in the shade of the trees, most were sliced and dried - preserved for the winter. Whichever the case, the best-looking apples were the ones first to go. I quickly learned, however, that looks were deceiving. Countless times I was surprised to cut or bite open the shiny seal of skin to find a worm who had browned the once-white-insides. Sometimes I even bit directly into the worm! Spitting the apple out in dramatic fashion then chucking the fruit into the pasture followed. The cows and horses were happy, but for me, it was always a heart-breaking disappointment to find the most perfect-looking apple actually had terrible insides.

In 2023 a picture came to mind one day. It had been one of the worst years of my life. I had fallen into depression and was overwhelmed with anxiety. My faith was in question, but my identity in Christ had gone beyond that. "A loved child of God" - I didn't believe it anymore at all. So, lonely in my work office, a picture of an apple came to mind. It was my favorite kind - red but with highlights of yellows and greens. A short brown stem had a single, vibrant green leaf atop it. It appeared delicious, perfectly ripe. Then, to my surprise, when the apple was turned, a slimy, nasty worm was halfway through the skin, eating its way inside.

I realized immediately that I was that apple. From the front view, I was pretty. Anyone looking straight at me could see a beautiful young woman, good at her job, friendly to all, clean and well-dressed. No one would suspect that lurking just out of view, a grubby monster was wreaking havoc. While this picture (you may call it a vision if you like) was disturbing to me, I continued to live the rest of 2023 in the same state. After all, I thought, how much damage could one, little worm do?

It took months, and many sacrifices on my loved-ones, for me to discover the damage was catastrophic. Metaphorically, you could even say it took being sliced open by those who truly cared about me, for me to gaze upon the destruction of my insides that finally opened my eyes. I was near death - truly hospitalized by a panic attack and placed under suicide watch - when the overwhelming reality of my situation hit. I was decaying. From the inside out, I was dying. That tiny, little worm I had once viewed as simple-enough, had tricked me. His innocent appearance was a lie. He had no plans of eating a few bites and moving on. He was going to consume all of me until there was nothing left, that selfish little larva.

Dispelling my worm was not an easy task, but the healing that followed was miraculous. The year is 2024 and I am living in freedom. I am eager to share with you the lessons I learned through that vision of the apple. It is my hope that worms in your life are exposed and dispelled. It is my prayer you experience healing through the Savior Jesus. It is my desire you taste and see that the Lord is good, and when His goodness is in you, you taste good too (Psalm 34:8).[1]

Let me preface this book by saying that all metaphors break down. I'm attempting to build an entire book off one illustration. Not everything is going to be perfect. You and I will run into gaps in my allegories. At the end of it all, know that the main message is found in the Gospel. Jesus loves you. Indeed, I am presenting nothing new. All this information you can find in other books. You can find it written by theologians with way more credentials, psychiatrists with way more research, and so on and so on. So give me grace. Find the nuggets of truth within these words that God wants to speak to you, and enjoy.

---

[1] All Scripture references are NLT or NIV unless noted otherwise.

Illustration of the vision.
By Kamra Smith

Chapter 1
Apples

"In the beginning God created the heavens and the earth..." (Genesis 1:1) He created land, dirt, soil, mud, sand, rocks. He created seeds. Seeds of all kinds. Some grow into flowers, some into bushes, some into trees. Some of these trees produce lemons, some walnuts, some have leaves good for teas, and some can be tapped for syrup. Regardless of the shape, size and color, everything He made He did purposely, and for a purpose.

Let's take one creation for example. Oh, let's go with apples and see where it takes us. Apples were created on purpose and for a purpose. What is their purpose? To be enjoyed of course! They certainly have the ability to reseed and become a tree providing shade and more apples, but even in that state, they are still fulfilling their primary purpose - being enjoyed. They simply get to hang around, basking in the sunshine. What a life! O, to be an apple!

You & I = Apples

Hi, my name is Kamra and I am just like an apple. I too was created purposely and for one purpose: to be enjoyed by God and to enjoy God in return. My function is to hang around, soaking up the Son. Don't worry; I don't use that as an excuse to sit around all day and eat sun chips. Knowing that this is my primary purpose gives me a passion for finding Jesus in all that I do, see and hear. It drives me to want to share the Son's goodness with all those around me. My life is not picturesque of a couch potato. However, my life is easy in the sense that I don't have to work for God's favor. I don't have to work to earn anyone's favor. My happiness is not driven by other's approval or an amount of material possessions. This may not always be true of my thoughts and actions, as I have had my fair share of seasons of drought and doubt. But ultimately, I know this is my truth and I try to live it. It is the truth of every Christian, every believer born in Christ who has entrusted their life to Him.

The Westminster Shorter Catechism answered the question, "What is the chief end of man?" this way: "To glorify God and to enjoy him forever."[2] When Adam and Eve were created they weren't done so with a to-do list tacked to their thigh. There were no expectations upon them, but that they be happy there in the Garden of Eden with God. One may interject here that procreation was an expectation, but if you've done any procreating yourself (accidental or purposely) you may note that it can be kind of enjoyable. So I stand by my statement that there was no real stressor on them to work or do anything that may not be enjoyable for all involved. I'll also add the reminder that this was pre-curse. There was no terrible pain to be had during labor or delivery. It was all fun and all reward!

It may also be interjected here that Adam and Eve did have a rule. One single rule - not to eat of the Tree of the Knowledge of Good and Evil. Still, this rule wasn't one to stifle their fun; it was a rule to protect them and ensure their enjoyment. All God had in mind, from the very beginning, was to love and to be loved in return.

It is for this purpose, you and I were created - to be loved. It is this reason that everything was created - to show God's love. What other purpose does an apple

---

[2] *Westminster Assembly (1643-1652). The Assembly's Shorter Catechism, with the Scripture Proofs in Reference : with an Appendix on the Systematick Attention of the Young to Scriptural Knowledge, by Hervey Wilbur. Newburyport [Mass?] :Wm. B. Allen & Co., 1816. https://prts.edu/wp-content/uploads/2013/09/Shorter_Catechism.pdf*

have other than to provide nutrition to those who consume it? Even if it were planted in the ground and became a tree, it is functioning as a beautiful piece of nature that provides nutrition, shade, clean oxygen and - dare I say it - even firewood for the warmth of man. The apple was created just to show us God loves us. The same logic can be applied to all of creation. Mountains, flowers, penguins and peacocks, wind, waves, caves, cantaloupes and antelopes... Every created thing can serve an incredible purpose in how the world functions, but their overall purpose is the same - demonstrating to humans that there is a God who loves us and created all of this so we could enjoy Him.

To think that our life was once created to be lived as simply as an apple hanging in a tree is almost too far-fetched to imagine. We've become so accustomed to believing our worth is determined by performance and our paths must be marked by accomplishments clothed in complements, that we can't wrap our minds around a simpler life. A life that does not hinge on the approval of others sounds too good to be true. A life whose worth is not measured in money, success, material possessions or accolades, is nearly bizarre to comprehend. It is quite sad that we humans can't imagine a world where we simply walk with God in a garden and enjoy each other's company. It is sadder still to think that could have been our reality if not for one stupid worm.

You may be familiar with the Genesis story. If not, I recommend you stop now to read the first three chapters of the Bible. Our perfect paradise was ruined when the Serpent, whom I will often refer to as a worm, deceived Eve and she acted upon his lies. "Did God really sssssssssssssssay...?" he hissed at her (Genesis 3:1). He was slithering around in the one tree that God had warned them not to eat from. Back then women had no reason to be afraid of snakes. Back then they supposedly didn't crawl on their bellies and likely were not carnivorous (Genesis 3:14). So this serpent of old was not a scary python most of us would run away from screaming like little children. Not to Eve anyway. He was just another one of God's critters, hanging around, with a tickly tongue and curly tail. Eve did not see danger when she saw the serpent. She saw what we would today - just a worm, a harmless, little worm.

Pretty crafty of that Tempter, wasn't it? To take on this form. He knew what he was doing. He didn't want to appear frightening. He wanted to appear as a friend, harmless and innocent, with only the best intentions in mind. He had to appear this way, that way he could get close. He had to draw Eve over to the tree that she had no business messing around.

How fascinating it was for Eve to hear words that were unlike her best friend's (that's God) and her husband's (Sir Adam). Imagine, if you will, a world where everyone shares the same opinion but one person. Just one solitary person. Even if they were greatly outnumbered, and even if everyone else was in agreement, that one person would still draw a lot of attention. Eve was drawn to the serpent because he was the only one speaking something contrary. The urge to discover if it was a lie or truth was tempting. So that stinking, slippery, lying son of a snake tripped Eve up, and he's been doing it to you and I ever since.

Why he would want to spend his days doing such a thing will be further explained in the next chapter, but let me make it plain here: Satan wants to kill us because we are God's workmanship.

Satan = Hates God

God = Loves Us

Therefore

Satan = Hates Us

The earth has the amazing honor of displaying God. Everything around us proclaims His handiwork. The palm trees bow down. The trees applaud in the wind. The ocean demands He has a manifesto. The galaxy paints his majesty. On and on, every creature, every plant, animal and every stone has a voice that sings God is the orchestrator of the world's choir.

Since Satan hates God, every note of worship is a painful reminder of who He is and why we are here. He is determined to shut us up. He is determined to make this beautiful place as ugly and insufferable as possible even though that is not why it was created. Romans 1:20 tells us, "Since the creation of the world his invisible attributes, his eternal power and divine nature, have been clearly seen because they are understood through what has been made. For this reason, people are without excuse." This earth and all that is on it was created to show God's beauty and purpose, His love and pursuit of us. We all are supposed to be able to look around and see God's fingerprints.

Unfortunately, many people look around and use what they see as an excuse not to believe in a good God. They see pain, suffering, starving children, sexually abused girls, devastation, natural disasters, and the like as reasons for if a God does exist, that he must be evil or careless. It is ironic when all of it was created so we could see God's true character. But that is precisely why it is under attack.

Satan's daily task is to make this world a little bit uglier. He wants the people on it to be a little closer to death and further blinded to see the goodness of God. So he gets to cluttering. He gets to messing. Like a raccoon who wants to pull out every piece of garbage from the dumpster, he starts pitching. He goes into town and causes a fuss. He stirs up trouble. He rallies people into protests. He forms brothels. He possesses men to steal from children. He kicks up the dust so we can't see clearly the beauty that is just beyond.

Rather than seeing the good that is in the world, we have a knack for seeing all the negatives. We're a pessimistic people. We can mosey through miles of peaceful meadows but spot the sinkhole. We can drive for hours through scenic byways but complain about the potholes. We can stand at the foot of a mountain but stare at a pile of trash. Satan is at work in making a world of cynics. Where we are meant to see God staring back at us, Satan wants to put a distraction right between.

If I asked you to, I bet you could look out your window and find something that is of beauty. A singing bird, perhaps. Maybe your dog. Could there possibly be a landscape that is delivering to you a message of tranquility?

I venture to ask you this because I guarantee we can still see the true character of God, loving and beautiful, beneath all the rubble and chaos Satan has caused. We can still see that it is a world designed gracefully. We just need to strip it back down to its origin. We need to clear out the clutter and crud Satan has distracted us with. We have to get back to the basic question: What was I and it all created for?

When Adam was created he was given the honor of naming all the animals (Genesis 2:19-20). He got to be a caretaker. He got to be a creator. He was acting out the image of God just as he was created to do. He was making things and giving things identity. He was doing what God had done with him. This is what we were intended to do. We were made to be godly. We were made to show all other creatures they were created by God; therefore, seen and appreciated.

I had the great honor to grow up on a farm. I learned so much from my gardening momma and my cattleman daddy. I was taught that the earth is precious. Dirt is valuable. Seeds are treasures. We tend to the ground. We till and hoe and pull up weeds. We water. We fertilize. We bottle-feed calves when the mommy's can't tend to their babies. We help them deliver when they are struggling to give birth. We provide them grain and fresh water. We work all year round to make sure they have enough hay to eat. We disc, mow, rake, bale, and pitch into haylofts. We start up the tractor even in the dead of winter. We break ice on the ponds. We vaccinate and give minerals. We keep them safe from coyotes and fence them in so they are always in our care. I could go on and on but this is what I'm getting at: As a farmer I learned the great honor of caring for God's creation because that is what He does and He is who I'm meant to be like.

There is a sweet reward like no other when you reap what you sow. The tomatoes taste better when you start them from seed. The cows taste better when you raise them on grass. The chickens taste better free range. The strawberries sweeter when tended and waited for. A great sense of pride fills the soul when you gaze upon the land bearing plentiful crops that you poured sweat and tears into. If you haven't ever farmed or gardened like that, you can still relate in other ways. You can feel that sense of accomplishment when you get the A on the paper you worked so hard on; when you eat the rolls you took so long to knead and bake; the applause after the performance you practiced for; the home run after all the batting cage practices, the child got into college that you raised . . . I'm sure you can think of something that meant all the more valuable to you when you had a hard-working hand in the development.

You and I were created to enjoy the goodness this earth has to offer. Before the fall Adam and Eve were directed to," Be fruitful and multiply. Fill the earth and subdue it. Rule over the fish of the sea and birds of the air and every creature that moves on the ground." God said, "I give you every seed-bearing plant on the earth and every tree that has fruit. They will be yours for food" (Genesis 1:28-30). Mankind was commissioned to take care of the planet and all that inhabit it. Like God, we were to see that it was good. We were to appreciate it. When we see animals that need tending, we care. When we see plants that need watered, we grab the hose. When we see a human hungry, we feed them. Etc. Why? Not because it is a chore and not because we have to. When we do these things we are satisfied. God gave us this longing when he made us in his image.

We-apples were made to bring joy to the world. We were created to make it a more beautiful place, not to destroy it or abuse it. We were made to foster the flowers. We-apples add a touch of color to this place. We are to be fragrant and sweet. We are not a rotten thing created to stink up the place. Even in our death and dying we were made to bring life. You'll hear more on this in the seed chapter. In the meantime, know that you and I were created for a marvelous purpose.

Hi, my name is Kamra and I'm wonderfully made by a good God. I see his mighty strength when I look up the tall trunk of a tree. I delight in him watching a bird take flight. I smile at his goodness when a baby is born. My mouth drops open at the Himalayan mountains and I could sit and stare at him at the ocean's edge for hours. His transformative power is revealed to me in butterflies.

His majesty through horses. His cute tenderness in bunnies and purring kittens. I worship the Creator alongside his creation. It is my privilege to do so. It is yours too. So I ask you, are you enjoying God?

Chapter 1 Reflection

1.   What were you created for?
2.   How are you living out your purpose?
3.   How have you complicated your purpose in life?

Get back to the basics of life - where you enjoy God.

Label the illustration.

Chapter 1 Challenge

Choose one of the three (Or all three if you're daring!) to complete:

1)   Purge
Clean out a space (your bedroom, your basement, your dorm room, your entire house, your garage, etc.).
Throw out or donate items that are cluttering, unnecessary, unused.
Meditate on this verse throughout:

He must increase.
I must decrease.
John 3:30

2)   Simply
If your schedule is busy this week or this month, look at what you can cross off. Instead of attending every event, make time to be still with the Lord.
Here are some examples of what you could do in that time instead:
Read your Bible, a devotional book, pray, listen to worship music, sit in the quiet and listen for God to speak, take a walk through nature and enjoy what God has made.
Meditate on this verse this week:

Be still and know that I am God.
Psalm 46:10

3)   Fast
For twenty-four hours choose something of importance to you to fast from.
Here are some examples of what you could fast from:
Food, snacking in between meals, any drink but water, television, your cell phone, screen time, social media.

During the times you would traditionally revert to that which you are fasting from, choose to meditate on this verse instead:

Make it your ambition to lead a quiet life:
You should mind your own business and work with your hands,
just as we told you, so that your daily life may win the respect of outsiders
and so that you will not be dependent on anybody.
1 Thessalonians 4:11-12

If you are doing this study with a small group, make time to discuss this challenge with them and encourage one another.

Chapter 2
The Worm

I recently sat in a small group discussion over the twenty-third Psalm. Since this is such a familiar passage of Scripture in Christian circles, I did not expect the conversation to spiral into deep apologetic questions. But verse 5 - "You prepare a feast before me in the plain sight of my enemies..." - took us down a rabbit hole of why God created the enemy in the first place. Questions ping-ponged around the group like, "Why did God create Satan if he knew what was going to happen?" and, "Why does God let Satan continue to pester us?"

Perhaps you are in the same place as you begin to read this book. Maybe you are already waving your hands saying, "Wait a second! God created me - an apple - to just enjoy him, but it doesn't seem we have a fair chance at doing that when worms are looking to eat us! Why would God let them exist? Back up, Kamra!" Okay, you got it. Let me take a quick step back to explain why there are worms in the first place. Please don't expect a thorough analysis of each Scripture reference, as entire books have been devoted to the origin of sin, Satan, and the like. I recommend setting aside study time for this topic as well. Take a deep dive into the theological bowels of "sin, suffering, and Satan." In the meantime, I'll give you a quick dunk.

When we begin reading the Bible we may be startled when we come upon Genesis 3:1. The first two chapters go into detail of how God created the world. There's a good bit of time spent describing the Garden of Eden and how God made Adam and Eve specifically. Chapter two ends on such a happy note: "The man and his wife were both naked, but they were not ashamed"

(Genesis 2:25). They were in complete bliss. They were butt naked, without a single worry of getting a bug bite on their butt cheek or poison ivy up their crack. What a wonderful, nude world! Then, suddenly, there's a shrewd serpent telling them their lives aren't actually perfect and the whole thing is a sham. Where did he come from?!

Unfortunately, the Genesis account does not give us all the answers. We see from the curse that God lays on the serpent that this is an enemy who will continue to be in hostility with us. His demise is prophesied, but his creation is not clarified (3:15). We don't actually get the whole picture until we see it in past, present, and future tense - through the vision received by John - written in the book of Revelation.

The apostle John was given remarkable visions near the end of his life on earth. He records that God told him in a loud voice, "Write down what you see and give it to the seven churches" (Revelation 1:11). One after another, he recounts visions after visions that came to him while on the island of Patmos. One day, he has a vision that incorporates three different signs. These visions are like pictures in the grand scheme of the whole vision. Like segments of a movie taken and placed in a trailer, they encapsulate the main idea but may not put everything into an order that the viewer may understand. This trailer certainly catches the audience's attention and gives a good idea of what it is all about, but they cannot put everything that will happen in the entire movie together based on the short scenes that are compiled. So let's look at some of John's scenes.

The three signs John receives are of a woman, a child, and a dragon. (Read Revelation 12)

The First Sign - The Woman

The scenes with the woman show one of royalty, giving birth to a son. She is put in a land God prepared for her; however, it is a land where a dragon chases her. She's given protective measures against the dragon, successfully birthing many more children, but remaining in a hostile environment. These additional children "keep God's commandments and hold to the testimony of Jesus."

The Second Sign - The Child

The child is a male who is said to "rule over all the nations with an iron rod."At one point, he is caught up to God and his throne.

The Third Sign - The Dragon

Huge, red, and angry, this dragon is first seen as sweeping its tail so that a third of the stars fall from heaven to earth. In another scene he is standing before the woman waiting to eat whatever child she births. Again, in another scene, the dragon is in heaven fighting against angels. He loses the battle and is cast down from heaven to earth, along with his angels. John hears a loud voice in heaven saying the huge dragon - the ancient serpent, the one called the devil and Satan, who deceives the whole world - "has come down to you! He is filled with terrible anger!" When the dragon realizes he's been thrown down to earth where the woman is, he chases her. He even rallies a serpent to try to drown her. When the serpent fails at that, the dragon gets all the more angry and decides to wage war on all her other children. The scene ends with the dragon standing on the seashore.

There is no question who the dragon represents in John's vision. He is identified in 12:9 as the "ancient serpent, the one called the devil and Satan, who deceives the whole world." The first descriptor of this dragon harks all the way back to their first known encounter with him, thus the adjective "ancient." He is the olden snake of Genesis 3. He arrived there by falling from heaven. Jesus testifies that He saw it take place. Luke 10:18, "I saw Satan fall like lightning from heaven." Being a Trinitarian God, Jesus was there with the creation of Satan, saw his rebellion, the war, and watched him be cast down to earth. From the moment he landed, he has been a tyrant. That is why Jesus describes him as the "ruler of the earth" (Ephesians 2:2); Paul as "the prince of the air" (John 12:31, 14:30); and Peter as "a lion who prowls around looking for others he may devour" (1 Peter 5:8). Doesn't that sound just like the dragon chasing the woman and her children?

Jesus makes it abundantly clear that Satan has been doing this from the day he landed. "That father of lies has been murdering from the beginning!" (John 8:44) He steals people's lives by selling them lies. That is why Jesus said, "The thief comes only to steal and kill and destroy." (John 10:10) Those who are deceived by his empty words become "sons of disobedience." (Ephesians 5:6) Like children of Abraham, there is a long lineage of children of the deceived. One by one they are being killed - devoured like an apple.

So we circle back to the questions asked in my small group about the origin of sin and why an enemy has to exist in the first place. Satan, and his wormy army, exists for the same reason you do. He was originally created as a Cherub Angel - a being designed to carry out special tasks for God and give him praise (Ezekiel 28:12-15). Like you and I, he was created to experience God's love, to hang in the presence of God like a Golden Delicious. Likewise, he was created with freewill. He elected to sour and gave up his divine calling so that he could become a mud-dweller.

It doesn't make any sense, does it? Why would someone choose to do that - abandon heaven, a perfect paradise and the presence of an all-loving God, taking off an outfit of royalty, to sink as low as living in slime? The only logical explanation is that Satan must have hated God that much. It couldn't be that he loved himself that much. Loving himself wouldn't look like resigning from the most rewarding job in the world, forfeiting an apartment in glorious Light, to selecting insect status and muck mansions. No, he doesn't love himself. There is no love in him at all. Only prideful, arrogant, rotten hatred. It is not reasonable to assume Satan thought he was choosing to love himself over God. He would have thought that one through. The math is too easy:

God = Love.

Me + God = Loving Myself.

Satan knew crossing God off meant crossing off love. He chose hatred, misery, and ugliness. Some may say only someone who does not know the amazing love that is God would choose anything else, but Satan knew God. He knew love and elected instead, for evil. No wonder we call him the devil.

The attack is personal for Satan. It is a good versus evil kind of fight. Satan is the archenemy of God. Therefore, his attack is first and foremost against God's people. The evil spirit named Satan is in opposition to the Holy Spirit indwelling the believers of Jesus. Like water and oil, they do not mix. The enemy is very clear in Satan's eyes. In the Garden, the serpent didn't slither after the squirrel. He squinted his slit-shaped pupils at Eve and Adam - those "made in the image of God" (Genesis 1:27).

Through Scripture we see that Satan is going after specific folks - God's children. Yea, one special child gets extra attention from Satan. Back to the Revelation 12 vision, we see there is one male child who gets the dragon's fervent attention. Since this child is also described as being caught up into heaven, we can narrow in on who this may be referring to... His name is Jesus!

Jesus and Satan were pitted against each other from the beginning. After the serpent is successful in tripping Eve and Adam, God curses him. The physical snake loses his legs so forevermore all snakes have to crawl on their bellies, eating dust and getting trampled under hooves. The spirit of the snake - Satan - also will get stomped under foot. Genesis 3:15, "I will put hostility between you and the woman and between your offspring and her offspring; he will stomp your head, and you will strike his heel." The first Messianic Prophecy of the Bible - the Protoevangelium. This was the warning to Satan about how his demise will come. It was the first proclamation of the Good News. Genesis 3:15 is the first glimpse at what the four Gospels will declare.

Satan was on the lookout from that moment forward for anyone resembling saving grace for God's people. Anyone experiencing the freedom of enjoying God was a bulls-eye. You ever wonder why the Old Testament is one trial after another, one war then another, one bit of slavery to another capture? God's people were identifiable, blessed beyond measure, glowing with joy despite despair, wealthy in hallelujahs while whips slashed their flesh, and so they were targets - walking, praying, singing, annoying to Satan, targets.

One particular example may come immediately to your mind - Job. This man's story is notorious for being one of the worst cases of suffering. If someone is experiencing a bad time in their life, they may still be hard-pressed to say their bad day is anywhere near the severity of Job's bad season. In a single day Job lost all his oxen, donkeys, sheep, camels, servants, his sons and daughters (Job 1:13-22)! Why? Because he was "blameless and upright, one who feared God and turned away from evil...He was the greatest of all the people in the east" (Job 1:1-3). And this annoyed Satan to no end! "If you weren't so good to him Job would curse you, God." Satan mockingly tested. Hell-bent on trying to get others to hate God, Satan began the task of inflicting pain.

In this particular story with Job, there are many who debate the status and function of Satan. Since the Hebrew word is not a proper name, but a title meaning "the satan" or "accuser", some refuse to draw a direct line between capital S - Satan, that serpent of old - and a spiritual being who attended God's company that day. Whichever side you sit on, this truth can be found in both places: there is a spiritual being (more than one in fact) whose main job is to roam about the earth, walking back and forth across it, identifying God's people as prey (Job 1:7).

That notion can scare people. No one likes to know they have an enemy determined to destroy them. It is unsettling, unnerving. It may cause you to want to look over your shoulder, sleep with one eye open. But I am not writing this book to cause you to worry about the forces of evil that are surrounding us all. I am writing this so you may know it is real and that you don't have to be afraid.

Please note this chapter is called "the worm." I didn't label it, "Devil - the Mighty Dragon," or "Satan - the Powerful Man-eater." I have called him a worm. I have identified him in such a way to illustrate that he is nothing great. He isn't someone worthy of accolades. The fact that he even gets a chapter in this book is kind of frustrating. So, you see, the balance is delicate. Compared to our Great God, Satan is a pitiful worm. Unfortunately, this worm causes a lot of damage to us apple-humans, so he must be addressed.

Addressed. Not feared.

Many years ago I had a dream. I was walking down the road I grew up on. I was a teenager. In the distance, atop a hill, I saw a large mound in the middle of the road. The Holy Spirit, who walked beside me, told me to keep going and not be afraid. So, I did. As I got closer I noticed the mound was a very large snake that was coiled in the center of my path. It was so large the mound was as tall as I. I paused in fear. The Holy Spirit nudged me. "Don't be afraid," He said. I bravely took steps forward. The snake came into better focus. It wasn't coiled into a perfect mound. It was twisted and knotted up as if it had gotten itself tangled. The body wriggled about as if it were trying to free itself. I never saw the head but the Holy Spirit nudged me to give it more space. "He can still trip you up," He warned me. I moved a little further away from the thrashing snake as I went around it to continue down the road. I chuckled as I did so, finding it humorous that a snake had managed to make such a mess of its own body.

I didn't understand all of that dream when I had it. Over the years I have learned more and more from it. I've been able to identify that dream as a message from God and one about what our enemy, Satan, is actually like. He is like a giant worm, a snake. He appears gigantic and some would want to stay as far away from him as possible, thinking he's a big deal. But in reality, he's a snake that has gotten himself into a terrible mess. He's in a large ball of knots from trying to trick people. All of his scheming has gotten him tangled. He's caught in his own web of lies. Turning his back on God was the biggest mistake of his existence. Every day since he's only gotten more and more messed up.

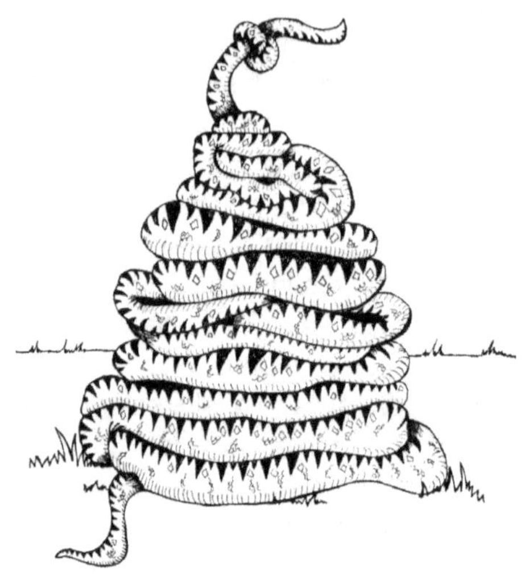

Illustration of the vision.
By Kamra Smith

Years after my dream I learned something else about that enemy I had seen. A section in a children's book about snakes caught my attention. It was titled, "How do snakes protect themselves?" Here's what it talked about: Some have the ability to camouflage so they blend into their surroundings. Prey will fly overhead or walk right by them without noticing. Others are striking colors so they fool their prey into thinking they must be venomous, even if they aren't. Some snakes are just incredibly fast. They can zip away from sight in a flash. Others have special gifts at escaping prey. The rattlesnake, for example, has a tail that rattles so loudly, the prey gets frightened away. The most humorous of the protective measures was "Playing dead." There are certain snakes that actually pretend to be dead so nothing will try to kill it. The hognose snake, for example, can actually roll over so its stomach is up in the air, and stick its tongue out as if it is dead! Crazy!

While flipping through this children's book with my infant, one other snake caught most of my attention. It is called the "rubber boa." This snake has the ability to curl into a ball and hide its head if attacked. Its protective measure is to curl up into knots to the point of having its own tail stick through the top of its mound to appear as its head. This way, if a predator tries to attack it, it will bite at its tail and not its own head. Pretty smooth, huh?

The illustration of this rubber boa took me back to the dream I had many years ago. A new realization came to me. That dreaded snake I feared in my path, that caused me to want to turn back, was actually scared of me. Or maybe I should say, the snake was scared of who was walking with me . . . Threatened by the presence of the Holy Spirit, that snake tucked its head and curled into a ball.

Do you know why Satan would want to tuck his head and hide? Because it is prophesied that his head will be crushed by Jesus. I believe Jesus actually did the stomping dance of damage when he was crucified and rose from the dead. With each pound of the hammer that drove the nails into his hands, a smashing blow came upon Satan. Then, when his stone was rolled away, it crushed the guts and brains right out of that Devil's head.

Now, with our King risen and seated on his throne, our snake of an enemy is headless but thrashing his body about. Just like in my dream. When we get close to Satan, the Holy Spirit warns us that his whipping tail can still sweep our feet out from under us. "Don't get too close," He nudges our hearts.

You see, Satan isn't a snake to be feared, but he's a snake that still wants to cause some damage. To keep along with our snake theme, let me put it this way: He's a constrictor.

Boa constrictors are snakes that squeeze the life out of their prey before they swallow them whole. If you've seen the classic movie Anaconda, you probably have really vivid images coming to mind when I say constrict. The word means, "to make narrower, especially through encircling pressure." It is death through asphyxiation. It is exactly what a noose does when tightened around a throat. It cuts off the air supply. It suffocates. Without breath, we all die. This is something I will expand on more in future chapters, so keep the importance of air in mind.

Satan wants to squeeze the air out of you. He wants you incapable of getting a breath of fresh air. He doesn't want you to have a moment of ease, to catch your breath. If given the chance, he will drown you. He will narrow in on you until darkness is all you see and pressure is all you feel.

A common way of describing depression is an inescapable amount of pressure on one's chest. I've heard it said it is like a big, black dog that lies on your chest. It feels unmovable. It makes it hard to breathe. Life is described as a burden that one can't push off. Now doesn't that sound like constriction? Depression, anxiety, stress . . . the disguises of a Satanic snake suffocating its prey.

Our enemy may be headless, but he is still dangerous. He is in the business of constricting one person after another and leaving them lay lifeless. Get too close, and this may be your fate. He'll wrap you into his mess and once you're in his grip, it'll be a heck of a fight to get loose.

The enemy doesn't want to let you go. Have you ever noticed misery loves company? Satan wasn't satisfied to hate God alone. He wanted others to join him. The metaphorical "swinging of the dragon's tail" swept one third of the angelic host to earth (Revelation 12:4). These fallen angels would become known as demons - Satan's minions. They too abandoned all that is loving when they elected to join Satan. They are not just fallen angels who happen to have chosen the wrong leader. They aren't spirits trapped on earth, innocently trying to win back God's favor. No, they are evil. Jesus identifies them as this. See Matthew 12:45. He says they are "evil spirits." In this particular passage he describes these evil spirits as those who like to possess people's bodies and leave it in a worse state. In other words, they want to get in people's bodies and destroy them from the inside out! Do these fallen angels sound like a pitiful little pest we must simply tolerate on our planet? No, to an apple's ears, they sound like some mighty terrifying worms!

Chapter 2 Reflection

1.   What is the Worm's purpose here?
2.   How has our enemy, The Worm, hindered our created purpose - to enjoy God?
3.   How do we have victory over the Worm?

The battle against the Worm is ongoing, but we know how the story ends!

Label the illustration.

Chapter 2 Challenge

Choose one (Or all three if you're feeling jazzed up!) to complete:

1.   Make a playlist of Christian music to listen to when you feel discouraged or under attack.
Here are some suggestions:Battle Belongs By Phil Whickham; Surrounded By The Upperroom; Praise By Elevation Worship; Victory in Jesus Hymn.
Listen to the words. You could even write down lyrics that touch you and put them in places you could frequently see them (your dashboard, the bathroom mirror, the fridge).

2.   Read Genesis 1-3.
I suggest printing out the passage and writing all over it. For example: Highlight what stands out to you; underline what God says; circle participants in the story; ask one question of the passage and search for the answer.

3.   Read the book of Revelation.
I know this is a hefty challenge but the text says, "Blessed is the one who reads the words of this prophecy and blessed are those who hear and obey the things written in it, because the time is near!" (1:3)
If you want to really understand why the Worm is here and how he gets squashed by our Savior, read the book and study it. You may not understand it all, but guess what, there is blessing in the reading! Ask for the Holy Spirit to help you along, and maybe some wise friends as well.
        If you are doing this study with a small group, make time to discuss this challenge with them and encourage one another.

Chapter 3
Worms

I grew up with three apple trees in the backyard. Multiple springs my family fought these nasty worms who made spider web-looking nests in the trees. A pocket of white silk would hang in the branches. If you looked closely enough you could spot little black bodies incubating in the mass. When they emerged they were spindly black and yellow furry creatures. I always assumed they were the culprits responsible for the holes in all our apples, but they actually weren't. This type of worm - often called Tent Caterpillars (because of the nature of their nests) - actually only eat leaves of fruit trees. If left untreated, they could kill a whole apple tree. The years these guys decided to nest in our trees would yield a weaker harvest of apples. They would feast on the leaves, turning them from a beautiful green to a speckled yellow color, half eaten and scrawny. With fewer leaves, the tree absorbed less sunlight. It became unhealthy. The apples it produced would be small and sour. They certainly did damage to our apple population, but not like the worms I'm trying to draw an illustration to now. The worms I'm talking about are the Codling Moth Caterpillars.

Codling Moth Caterpillars don't leave behind blindingly obvious nests that look like tents suspended in an apple tree. No, these worms are crafty. That is why I never suspected them as the apple-eaters. I didn't even know they existed. I blamed the Tent Caterpillars. Now I know the names of all those worms I bit or cut into all those days - it was the Codling Moth pre wing stage.

As all moths and butterflies do, the Codling Moth begins its life as a caterpillar. Hatched from an egg, these worms quickly crawl to find a source of food. In order to survive these tiny creatures must get inside a fruit as quickly as possible. If left exposed, they can easily fall from the tree branch, be washed off with the rain, gobbled up by a bird or larger insect, or even dry up in the sunlight. They are born with an instinctive mission - find fruit.

Their entire being relies on being able to find and feast on fruit; therefore, discovering it is of the utmost importance. How do they find it? Through a little means called phototaxis. This is a term used to describe a creature that uses light to navigate. A lot of winged insects are like this. Have you ever noticed a community of night bugs that congregate around your front porch light? Some insects are drawn to it. You know the old expression "like a moth to a flame"? This is true for the Codling Moth as well. As a baby caterpillar, it uses its senses to be drawn closer to the light. Why? Fruits grow where they are exposed to light. Indeed, the biggest and best fruits grow where they have the most light.

Within 24 hours of being hatched, a codling moth caterpillar, if not dead, has found its fruit. For the life of one sweet crispy little apple, a codling moth caterpillar is a death sentence. If an apple had eyes and could see this worm inching its way down a branch, it would see its life flashing before its eyes - the end of days. If it had a mouth, the apple would yell, "The Grim Reaper is approaching!" If I had known these worms were responsible for killing my favorite fruit, I would have been perched on branches with a magnifying glass. Alas, I couldn't protect my apples back then. I didn't know. The worms, being pale yellow, were nearly invisible to the eye. And they moved quickly. These worms were slipping right under my radar and landing later in my mouth.

Simple awareness could have given me the skills needed to defeat those worms that tormented my family apple trees all those years. There would have been less apples suffering. There could have been a lot less waste. There could have been a lot less gagging on my part. I just lacked the education; therefore, the action.

This won't be your story. When it comes to worms that want to attack your life, I want you to have the knowledge. I want you to be prepared. I want you to recognize the codling moth caterpillars inching closer to your stem, closer to your family and friends. Together, we can start calling them out - "Not today, Grim Reaper!" Let's take our eyes off distractions. Stop pointing fingers at tent caterpillars and let's name the real enemy.

Demons

When the dragon was in heaven, battling against angels and God, he swung his tail and took with him one third of the starry host; namely, he and a third of the angels were cast down to earth from heaven. Somehow other angels were persuaded to follow along with Satan and his plans to combat God. Some speculate Satan was so beautiful, angels were drawn to him. They were manipulated to follow him as if he were the pretty, popular girl in school. In a controversial passage I mentioned in the previous chapter, Ezekiel 28, he is described as perfect in beauty, covered in every precious stone (ruby, topaz, emerald, chrysolite, onyx, jasper, sapphire, turquoise, and beryl), his setting being made of gold. Captivated by this beauty, other angels may have elected to side with the Cherub Angel Satan. With him as their ringleader, they succumbed to the consequences of his leadership. They gained nothing, and lost everything.

A third of heaven's angels chose to be on Satan's team. He captains them in their game of hating God. If you were to be a fly on the wall of their locker room, you'd find Satan in the pit of hell, his ball cap of fire on backward, screaming at his demon defensive line, "Charge at the Christians! They're playing for God's team and we hate Him! We have to crush them all! Play dirty! Swipe the knee! Grab the facemask! Anything! Everything! Wipe the turf from your jersey with their blood! Leave no survivors!" Then to the offensive line he'd swing his pointy triton, "Take my message of hate down the field! God's angels are going to try to stop you, defending their precious Christians, but I say to you we must find a way! Be tricky! Memorize all my plays! Sneak up the sidelines! Anything! Everything!"

What makes this locker room picture all the more threatening is that Satan and his demons already know who wins the game. (See Revelation 20:7-10 for the Dragon's final defeat.) Some may think then that the logical response would be for Satan to not even fight. If you knew you were going to lose a game, would you even suit up? But this is not the mindset of someone completely driven by hatred. Satan, even while he knows the final victory is God's, goes to the field driven by rage, determined to inflict as much damage as possible to the opposing team while he still can. "God's got the win in the bag, huh?" Satan thinks to himself. "Then I'm going to try to leave Him with as few players as possible. I'm going after the quarterback, then the second string quarterback, then the third and fourth and so on. I'll make it as hard as possible to get this win. In the end God can have the trophy, but if I have anything to do with it, there won't be many people in heaven for him to share it with. If I can't be there at the victory party, then no one can!"

Knowing it is prophesied that he will lose doesn't deter Satan from fighting. It makes him fight all the harder. The demons are on the same page. They don't want to simply see you get sacked. They want to break your arm so you can't throw straight ever again. Don't believe for one second that demons are pouting on the bench - "What is the point in trying? We already know we've lost." No. They're wearing spikes on the souls of their cleats, horns on their helmets and fire is in their eyes.

Satan and his demons don't want to trot through this life and tailgate with you. They want to kill you or at least take you out of the game, carried off the field on a stretcher. They don't want to see you collaborating with teammates, making plays, cheering each other on, getting refreshed with water, and they definitely don't want you to study their moves, become aware of their plays and thus be able to slip on by with the pig-skinned gospel tucked under your arm.

In other words: Demons don't want unity within the church and amongst believers. They want to cause dissension. They want to cause confusion and bring impurity into the Church. They don't want Christians to agree there is one body, one Spirit, one Lord, one faith, one baptism, one God and Father of all (Ephesians 3:4-6). They don't want Christians spurring each other on toward love and good deeds (Hebrews 10:24-25). They want believers to stop gathering together. They despise Sunday worship services, Wednesday night children's ministry, vacation Bible schools, Sunday school, Monday night small groups, Christmas Eve candlelight services, live nativities, conferences, retreats, revivals, lock-ins, pitch-ins, young ladies group, men's associations, all of it! They want us to stop doing stuff. They want us to get lazy. They want us out of shape. They want us not to be able to run down the field when we're tossed the ball of Truth.

They don't want us to have these group gatherings because it is there that we all cheer each other on. We meet up for coffee and devotionals and start encouraging each other. We lay hands on one another and healings take place. The damage the Demon Linebacker tried to do Pastor Charlie's leg could be miraculously healed! The bout of depression the Demon Cornerback had been working on Deacon Alex could be cured! Demons can't let this happen! They fling their helmets in fury when a bottle of anointing oil appears. Fumes roll from their shoulder pads when they spot that study guide. Imagine the anger demons feel when they see Christians huddle together, agree with all hands in and reemerge to the field rejuvenated. "Just when I thought I got that one down," Demon Safety thinks, "they all lift him back up."

During team gatherings Christians get to lift each other up, but they also get lifted up by their coach - God. In His locker room, His spirit of peace wafts over every sweaty player and dries them up. He hands to each of them a bottle with the Water of Life. He gets to point to His Son, jersey #1, and say, "Jesus has taken the biggest beating out there. He was on the frontline. Look at His scars. Through Him you already have the victory in the bag. You just need to keep pressing on till the end. I, your coach, am not leaving you out there on the field defenseless. My guardian angels are battling alongside you." He goes on to tell you how valued you are. He leads you beside quiet waters and makes you rest in fields of green (Psalm 23). Pep talks in His locker room are the absolute best. After a few quiet moments with Him, listening to His Word, you can feel completely new, ready to rush the field again. The enemy does not want you to take a timeout with God.

More than anything, demons don't want you to become aware of their plays. Let me take a moment here to give you a sidebar. Believe it or not, I'm not a sports gal. My knowledge of football would make any loyal fan of the sport shake their head in shame. I faithfully watch the super bowl every year. In full disclosure, I do it for the snacks. But I know enough about football to know that the best way for a team to beat another is to study them. Hours can be spent watching footage. Stats are programmed to memory. Plays are watched, then watched again. I would bet good money coaches spend as much time watching old games as they do preparing for upcoming games. All this to say, it doesn't take a sporty girl to know a good tactic is to know who you are playing against. So to get off my sidebar, demons don't want you to know them. When Christians get together to hear and study the Word of God, they discover the way demons play.

Since Christians are the ones who ought to know the true awful character of demons, they are the ones who pose the biggest threat to Satan and his work here; therefore, Christians are the primary targets. Demons are attracted to them like moths to a flame, like caterpillars to the sunlight. The light of Christ illuminates from them like a lighthouse on the shore signaling to hungry worms, "Here's a tasty meal. This way!"

You could think of it like this: If an army found out a certain group of individuals had discovered their plan of attack, the army would first go after this group to keep their plan veiled and maintain the possibility of winning their war. Christians possess the enemies' battle plans. They have the Word of God.

Unfortunately, Christians who spend little to no time reading and studying the Bible are more likely to be unaware of the war that is raging around them. Take me for example. In 2023 my Bible study had dwindled to scraps. I wasn't bulking up on the Bread of Life. I was nibbling here and there at my Bible app. The times I did spend reading my Bible I wasn't allowing the Holy Spirit to speak to me. I was rushing through a chapter at a time just so I could say I had done it. My mind wouldn't even register the things I had read. I was like the man who looked in the mirror but would immediately forget his appearance when he turned away (James 1:23-24). Because of this neglect, I became more susceptible to the enemy's attacks. I wasn't concerned about them because I wasn't reading about them like I used to. The more time I spent away from the Bible, the more I lost recognition of the battle being fought for my soul. With my back turned to the Enemy, eyes off the Word, flaming arrows were freely being shot into my back.

In the book of Ephesians, Paul gives an exhortation to the followers of Christ about spiritual warfare. "Our battle is not against flesh and blood," he warns them. "Our battle is against the schemes of the devil, against the rulers of this darkness, against the spiritual forces of evil in the heavens; therefore, put on the full armor of God" (6:11-12). He goes on to draw an illustration between armor and spiritual disciplines. Truth is like a belt. Righteousness is like a breastplate. Peace is fitted to your feet like sandals. Faith is a shield. Salvation is a helmet. The book of Isaiah adds a cloak of zeal (59:17). All of these pieces are for the protection of the Christian. The shield of faith, for example, is given so the warrior can deflect the flaming arrows of the evil one. These pieces do not equip the warrior to fight back, only to withstand the fight coming against them. Please, also note, there is no article of armor to cover up a Christian's backside. This is because a Christian isn't meant to turn and run from the Enemy or whenever a difficult situation arises. If they do, they'll be like I was - getting arrows plunged into my back. No more. Christians, turn and prepare for battle.

There is only one article mentioned in Paul's list of the armor of God that equips the Christian to fight back - the Sword. "Take up the helmet of salvation and the sword of the Spirit (which is the Word of God)" (Ephesians 6:17). The best weapon to fight Satan and his army is the Bible. Since he and his demons know how Revelations ends, they don't just see a butter knife poking at them when you throw Scripture their way. They see a blade with their blood and guts already dried on it.

The Word of God is the perfect weapon to use against them. They cannot fight against it because the end is already written. It is unchangeable. It is factual. It is the spirit-breathed, hand-written description of their Conqueror and Creator. It is the flesh they tried to crucify in Word format. It is the light in the darkness that the darkness cannot overcome. When you fight using the Word of God, you fight demons with Jesus. Against Him, they do not stand a chance.

When Jesus physically walked the earth, he did hand to hand combat against the Enemy. That is why John wrote, "Now the Word became flesh and took up residence amongst us." (John 1:14). As a walking, talking sword, everything He did was the Word of God. When Satan personally attacked Jesus in the desert after fasting for 40 days, all Jesus had to do to fend him off was speak a little bit of truth about Himself. The crafty little worm tried to manipulate Jesus by throwing out some descriptors of God too, quoting Psalm 91:11-12. "This is what Scripture says about you..." the devil told him at the top of the temple. Jesus shook His head. "You're trying to take pieces of me out of context. You think you know me better than I know myself? Don't test me, Worm" (John 4:6-7). Ultimately, Jesus showed Satan he couldn't take pieces of the sword to try to cut Him. Jesus didn't use a tip here, the butt of the blade there, a tiny sliver of an edge there. The spirit-slaying power of the Word is only when it is whole, in full context, not broken into pieces to fit any situation desired. It is so powerful, Satan wanted to use just one tiny piece to try to gash Jesus. Imagine how threatened he is by Christians who know the Word front to back, who know Jesus inside and out.

Simply speaking the name of Jesus can cut the enemy down to size. When you read the Gospels you will notice how easily Jesus overpowered demons. In every encounter, Jesus needs only to say a few words, just a sentence, to the demons before they run in fear. Let's take a look through Mark just for giggles.

1:24-25 "Leave us alone, Jesus the Nazarene! Have you come to destroy us? I know who you are -the Holy one of God!" But Jesus rebuked him: "Silence! Come out of him!"

3:11-12 Whenever the unclean spirits saw him, they fell down before him and cried out, "You are the Son of God." But he sternly ordered them not to make him known.

5:6-13 When the demon possessed man saw Jesus from a distance, he ran and bowed down before him. Then he cried out with a loud voice, "Leave me alone, Jesus, Son of the Most high God! I implore you by God - do not torment me!" (For Jesus had said to him, "Come out of that man, you unclean spirit!") Jesus asked him, "What is your name?" And he said, "My name is Legion, for we are many." He begged Jesus repeatedly not to send them out of the region. There on the hillside, a great herd of pigs was feeding. And the demonic spirits begged him, "Send us into the pigs. Let us enter them." Jesus gave them permission. So the unclean spirits came out and went into the pigs. Then the herd rushed down the steep slope into the lake, and about 2,000 were drowned in the lake.

9:25-26 Jesus rebuked the unclean spirit, saying to it, "Mute and deaf spirit, I command you, come out of him and never enter him again." It shrieked, threw him into terrible convulsions, and came out.

See how easy Jesus defeated demons? He never showed an ounce of fear - not even in the face of men who needed to be chained in cemeteries, or of seizures, or foaming at the mouth. He didn't sweat it because He knew who they were and He knew who He was. Why would a mountain fear a boulder?

All this talk about demons and reading about possessions can frighten people. It can make the hairs on your neck stand up, the goose bumps pop up on your arms. But this chapter is not to make you fear demons. It is not meant to prompt you to keep an eye over your shoulder. This chapter should do the opposite. This chapter should show you what a mighty force you have on your side, sitting right beside you, laying by your bedside or on your bookshelf. You have the Word of God available to you. It is the world's best seller. You can find it in nearly every store, and in every hotel room. And even if you don't have a physical copy on hand, you have been gifted the Holy Spirit. You have Jesus in you at all times. His Word can be scrolling across your heart-screen 24/7. So, should you fear?

If you're still wondering how to answer that last question, maybe you need a quick recap on the kind of Jesus you have at your disposal. Just how sharp is he? Let's look through Matthew just for giggles.

4:11 Then the devil left Jesus and angels came and began ministering to his needs.

4:23-24 Jesus went throughout all of Galilee, teaching in the synagogues, preaching the gospel of the kingdom, and healing every kind of disease and sickness among the people. So a report about him spread throughout Syria. People brought to him all who suffered with various illnesses and afflictions, those who had seizures, paralytics, and those possessed by demons, and he healed them.

8:2-3 A leper approached and bowed low before him, saying, "Lord, if you are willing, you can make me clean." He stretched out his hand and touched him saying, "I am willing. Be clean!" Immediately his leprosy was cleansed.

8:13 Jesus said to the centurion, "Go; just as you believed, it will be done for you." And the servant was healed at that hour.

8:14-15 Now when Jesus entered Peter's house, he saw his mother-in-law lying down, sick with a fever. He touched her hand and the fever left her.

8:16 When it was evening, many demon-possessed
people were brought to him. He drove out the spirits with
a word, and healed all who were sick.

8:26 Jesus got up and rebuked the winds and the sea,
and it was dead calm.

9:2, 6-7 Some people brought to Jesus a paralytic lying
on a stretcher. When he saw their faith, he said to the
paralytic, "Have courage, son! Your sins are forgiven."
Then he said to the paralytic - "Stand up, take your
stretcher, and go home." So he stood up and went
home.

9:20, 22 A woman who had been suffering from a
hemorrhage for twelve years came up behind him and
touched the edge of Jesus' cloak. . . When Jesus saw
her he said, "Have courage, daughter! Your faith has
made you well." And the woman was healed from that
hour.

9:18-19, 25 A leader came, bowed low before Jesus and
said, "My daughter has just died, but come and lay your
hand on her and she will live." Jesus and his disciples
got up and followed him. . . He went in and gently took
her by the hand, and the girl got up.

9:27, 29-30 Two blind men began to follow Jesus
shouting, "Have mercy on us, Son of David!" He touched
their eyes saying, "Let it be done for you according to
your faith." And their eyes were opened.

9:32-33 As they were going away, a man who was
demon-possessed and unable to speak was brought to

him. After the demon was cast out, the man who had been mute began to speak.

14:17-21 They said to him, "We have here only five loaves and two fish." "Bring them here to me," Jesus replied. He instructed the crowds to sit down on the grass. He took the five loaves and two fish, and looking up to heaven he gave thanks and broke the loaves. He gave them to the disciples, who in turn gave to the crowds. They all ate and were satisfied, and they picked up the broken pieces left over, twelve baskets full. Not counting women and children, there were about 5,000 men who ate.

14:25-27 As the night was ending, Jesus came to them walking on the sea. When the disciples saw him walking on the water they were terrified and said, "It is a ghost!" and cried out with fear. But immediately Jesus spoke to them: "Have courage! It is I."

15:28 Jesus answered her, "Woman, your faith is great! Let what you want be done for you." And her daughter was healed from that hour.

15:30-31 Many came to him bringing with them the lame, blind, crippled, mute, and many others. They laid them at Jesus' feet and he healed them. As a result, the crowd was amazed when they saw the mute speaking, the crippled healthy, the lame walking and the blind seeing, and they praised the God of Israel.

17:1-2 Jesus took with him Peter, James and John the brother of James, and led them up a high mountain. He was transfigured before them. His face shone like the sun, and his clothes became white as light.

17:26-27 Jesus said to him, "The sons are free but so that we don't offend them, go to the lake and throw out a hook. Take the first fish that comes up, and when you open its mouth, you will find a four drachma coin. Take that, give it to them for me and you."

20:30, 34 Two blind men were sitting by the road. When they heard that Jesus was passing by, they shouted, "Have mercy on us, Lord, Son of David!" Moved with compassion, Jesus touched their eyes. Immediately they received their sight and followed him.

21:19 After noticing a fig tree by the road Jesus went to it, but found nothing on it except leaves. He said to it, "Never again will there be fruit from you!" And the fig tree withered at once.

28:5, 9 An angel said to the women, "Do not be afraid; I know that you are looking for Jesus, who was crucified. He is not here, for he has been raised, just as he said..." Jesus met them saying, "Greetings!" They came to him, held on to his feet and worshiped him.

See how sharply powerful He is? He can heal the mute, the deaf, the lame, the paralyzed, the possessed, walk on water, calm storms, kill trees with a single touch and He can raise up from the dead! If he can conquer death, can he cast away a puny demon-worm? Of course, he can! You should not fear, brothers and sisters. This chapter about worms is not to scare you. It is to show you how incredibly pathetic they are in comparison to Jesus; therefore, you shouldn't let them be feasting on you! Utilize the power of Jesus that is within you and cast out the worms from your life.

Not only is Jesus on your side, but His own league of angelic warriors are fighting on your side too. When the dragon was cast out of heaven he took with him one third of the starry host. This means two thirds of God's angels are still on God's side - and yours! These angels, by the way, are not wimpy junior high guys you'd pick last for your kickball team. These angels are larger than life creatures. Don't believe me? Let's look at just one example - the angel at the tomb of Jesus.

Matthew 28 describes the resurrection of Jesus. The women had just gotten to the tomb when suddenly there was an earthquake, for an angel of the Lord came down from heaven and, going to the tomb, rolled back the stone and sat on it (Matthew 28:2). I love when my dad preaches on this topic. He likes to describe the angel as being so big and so strong that he needed only one finger to flick the heavy stone out of the doorway of the tomb. This is a stone that is so big it can block an entrance large enough for adults to walk through it. But for the angel, it was small enough to plop right down on top of it, like a footstool. This angel was so massive and so determined, when he landed on the ground, the ground wanted to give way.

His appearance was like lightning. What does that even mean?! I don't know about you, but when I see lightning strike I don't think, "What a cute little streak that just shot from the heavens and obliterated that tree." I think, "Take cover!" This angel's lightning appearance wasn't an exaggerated way of saying he was bright. It is a way to describe something fierce hitting the earth with a sparking impact. When the soldiers saw him they did think, "Take cover!" Only they were so scared they fainted before they could run.

Fainting at the sight of one of God's mighty angels is probably the most accurate response the human body could give. There's a reason angels always announce their presence with the opening statement: "Do not be afraid." They're probably lucky to get those four words out without having the recipient of their message black out.

These jaw-dropping, freeze you in your steps, nearly blind-you-bright, earth-moving angels are on your side. They stand with you when it is time to fight. They stand even when you can't. They guard you while you sleep. They take the blunt of the blows that you didn't know were swung. They're the ones you can thank when you come out of a situation saying, "How did I escape that?" They're invisible right now, but they are the most real friend to you, the most loyal servants to our God.

My dad says if we could see his guardian angel he would probably have a broken wing, a gimpy leg and missing fingers, toes and teeth from all the rough times he's gone through. It is a funny way to paint a picture of how God is providing provision for us, but ultimately we know that Jesus really did take the beating for us. He stood in the way of the devil's flaming arrows the day he was nailed to the tree on Golgotha. When you look at Him, you really will see a scarred man, holes in his hands and feet, and scars upon his back and side. On that day he could have called down twelve legions of angels to destroy the soldiers crucifying him, the Pharisees mocking him, and the doubters on-looking. Though he had the power to command them to come down that day, he didn't. Instead, he died so we could live with His Spirit. He fights alongside us and commands his angels to protect us. This is the beautifully-beaten, resurrection-restored Jesus we have on our side.

You know how the fallen angels of Satan are described? Throughout the New Testament the Greek word, ἀκάθαρτον, is ascribed to these spirits. It means unclean, impure or foul. It is the same adjective used to describe certain meats that Jews were not allowed to consume. The idea was that putting something like that into your body would defile you from the inside out. The same idea is ascribed to people in the Old Testament who needed to be cleansed from certain sins or diseases. Ceremonies like bathing seven times had to be done in order to purify themselves. It was a direct link between outward filth to a moral impurity.

When Jesus exercised a demon in the Gospels, this was the term used to describe those spirits. They were unclean. They were foul. I literally think of a stinky, smelly, downright gross creature. These demons are creatures that make you dirty. They rot you from the inside out. They are the disgusting worm that gets inside and turns your white core into brown mush. They defile everything they touch. When you encounter one you ought to feel the need to wash off, to scrub with soap and soak in a tub. When you're around them you should smell they are unclean, filthy beings. These spirits make you feel icky, sick to your stomach, and make you want to turn your head away as if a plate of garbage was stuck under your nose. This is how sin ought to make you feel, and these creatures are trying to stuff you full of it, to kill you in a sea of sin.

Do you see why God might not want a single thing to do with this kind of adjective - ἀκάθαρτον?[3] Do you see why Satan and his fallen angels had to be cast down from his presence? A holy God cannot tolerate such filth.

---

[3] All Greek references are taken from Strong's unless noted otherwise.
Strong, J. (2010). *The new Strong's expanded exhaustive concordance of the Bible* (Red letter ed.). Thomas Nelson.

Do you see why Jesus was determined to rid as many people as he could of their possession? Do you see why he didn't want them to have a single foothold over anyone? He didn't even want pigs to live with such unclean spirits in them. He gave the swine the honor of letting them die before having to live with such a creature inside them. Even mud-loving, slop-eating pigs went insane with such filthy spirits entering them. So, how do we - privileged and pristine - humans allow such unclean spirits into our lives?

Tragically, demons have the ability to disguise themselves. They can enter into pigs. He can take the form of a serpent. Together, they can use a lot of masks to make themselves appear clean, shiny, and desirable. Just as Satan tricked Eve and Adam into coming close to him, we all are in danger of letting a disguised, evil spirit into our presence. Recognizing them from a distance, before they do any damage, is a skill one can possess over time. Hopefully, this book (among others) helps you in that identification process. In the meantime, there is one sure way of knowing if that person or thing in your life is a worm. Just ask yourself this: "Is it killing me?"

Worms have purpose - eat, kill. They think only of themselves. They are feeding off us so they can continue to play their game of "destroy the orchard of God." Unfortunately, knowing if something, or someone, is killing you is not always an easy question to answer either. Someone chewing tobacco may be able to say, "It is not killing me," but they may not be aware of the long-term effects it may have on their body, like cancer - a human-killing machine.

Or take that sweet, innocent teenage girl for example. Upon meeting Joe Shmoe she may have imagined he'd be her perfect new beau. He was handsome and opened the door for her on their first date. He said all the right things to her dad. He bought her the sweetest valentine's day card. But below all the surface level things, he was demonizing her belief system. He started blaming their happiness on why she believed they shouldn't have sex before marriage. He pressured her and pressed her until she was convinced he had the right intentions. He told her he loved her. He flashed that adorable smile. He tenderly held her. How could he be bad for her? He was giving her all the things she thought she had wanted for so long. She was getting attention. She was getting it in a way she never had before. Surely, he was good and what she had once thought was right was what was wrong. So she gives him her body. She lets him in. It is the most personal thing she has ever let someone do to her because she believes he is good and definitely good-looking.

Fast forward. He dumps her. He's through with her. He leaves and finds another apple. She's ate through and left laying on her bed feeling like a rotten heap of flesh. Joe Shmoe says he never really loved her. He just wanted sex. And this once pure and darling apple is left wondering how she ever believed that worm was the best thing that would ever happen to her.

This is not to say that all relationships that involve sex and end up in separation was a wormy debacle. But this is a perfect example of how sin can look so right from the incoming angle and end up being a monstrous hurt upon its exit.

The way to determine if someone or something is going to damage you before you let it in is to ask where it is coming from and what its end goal will be. If I let chewing tobacco into my life, what will the consequences be? Will it in any way benefit me? If I let Joe Shmoe into my life, will he respect me and let me preserve what I value or try to change it? Is Joe Shmoe respective of my core values or is he someone that wants to rearrange my insides so there is more room for his wants and desires? These are not easy questions. I've said it once and I'll continue to say it: Self-reflection is not a walk in the park. Evaluating your health should not be a five-minute checkup. Sometimes we want to avoid taking a good look within because we're afraid of the damage we may find, or we don't want to accept that there is something that needs to be removed. Fixing things takes work and we are a lazy kind of creature. But I have good news for you followers of Jesus: When that worm is spotted we get to say, "You don't belong there. Jesus has ownership of me. Jesus take this worm away." And He does.

It is a downright shame when Christians think they have to do it all on their own, when they believe they have to rid the worm in order for Jesus to be with them. I shake my head in sadness when I think of all the people living trying to make themselves clean, or living with the false hope that they will never be good enough so don't even try.

While we might be thinking it is completely insane for Satan and demons to choose hatred and separation from the God of Love, the sad truth is, many of us are choosing the same. Any time we elect not to love God, we are selecting not to love ourselves and vice versa. We are choosing a path of hatred, misery and ugliness. It is for this reason that loving ourselves is included in the top two greatest commandments: 1) Love God; 2) Love your neighbor as yourself (Matthew 22:36-40). It is impossible to fully love God when we do not love ourselves or others.

It is another simple equation:

God made me.
God = Love
Therefore, God loves me and everyone else.
I love me and others because God = Love made me and everyone.
Therefore, when I love me and others, I am loving God.

Many of us apples have lost love for ourselves, or haven't ever fully found it to begin with. Therefore, we are accepting less and less of God, and more and more is being given, even taken, by the enemy. We look upon our apple-bodies and say, "Worms can have it." We don't feel worthy of anything else. We let ourselves be destroyed. When we do this we are disbelieving the capability of God to make things that are loved and loveable. I have to stop us right there. If you are someone that doesn't love yourself then you are not fully loving God. You are saying to Him that what He makes isn't that great. You are downplaying Him. It is like telling an artist that his painting isn't all that pretty. It makes him sad. If you want to show God maximum love, you look into the mirror and say, "You are a marvelous artist; therefore, I am a masterpiece. Me. With my mascara running from my tears. With the zit on my nose. With the scar on my forehead. With my past. With all of it. Still, it is marvelous." Please see yourself as such. If you don't, worms will take advantage of you all day long.

For some apples, self-love is not the hard part of that equation. The hard part is seeing other apples as loved and loveable creations. Still, we must view them as masterpieces. We must honor one another. When we esteem others we are awarding God. When we treat others less than we are helping the enemy in his hole-eating way of life.

We should all band together in the fight against hatred. We all ought to strive to love ourselves and to love each other, even our enemies. If we do that we will have the real enemy identified.

The Real Enemy

I am reminded of a scene from the Hunger Games: Catching Fire. Katniss turns on Finnick with her bow and arrow ready to shoot. He puts his arms up in surrender and says, "Katniss, remember who the real enemy is." At that moment her mind clears and she sees Finnick for who he really is. She remembers where she is. She's not simply in an arena. This is her life she is battling for. She turns her arrow to the sky and shoots at the real enemy surrounding her.

You and I have gotten distracted. We have forgotten who the real enemy is. We point our arrows at Finnick's instead of President Snow's. We point our fingers at Tent Caterpillars instead of the Codling Moth. We blame pawns instead of the demon lurking behind the disguise. We have to remember, "Our battle is against the schemes of the devil, against the rulers of this darkness, against the spiritual forces of evil in the heavens; therefore, put on the full armor of God" (6:11-12). We have been given the arrow of love. When we shoot it out we are killing off the real source of evil.

There was a time I wasn't loving myself well. I wasn't loving others well either. You could say I was distracted by pawns. You could say I had just given myself over to be eaten. You could say I was barely hanging on or I had even rolled away. Either way, a worm was eating me and I don't want this for you. I want you to acknowledge the worms of this life. I want you to love yourself and others. I want you to imagine me approaching you now, whether your defenses are up or not, and I say, "Reader, remember who the real enemy is. It is the Worm and his worms."

The remaining chapters of this book are going to use the illustration of an apple to help you recognize parts of yourself that may need further protection from the enemy. I'll call them soft spots and bruises. I'll explain there are areas within yourself that the enemy wants to destroy more so than anywhere else - your core and your seeds. Lastly, I'll explain some protective measures that are already here for you to utilize - the Farmer, the Orchard and Pesticides.

Hi, my name is Kamra and I love apples. Know what else? I hate worms. What say you?

Chapter 3 Reflection

1.   What are the worm's purposes here on earth?
2.   What "team"(s) can you say you are a part of? Reflect on your participation on the team of Christ. In what ways are you being a helpful teammate?
3.   Read Ephesians 6:11-12 aloud. What (or who) are pawns in your life the Enemy may be using to get under your skin?

Know who the real enemy is and STAND FIRM.

Label the illustration.

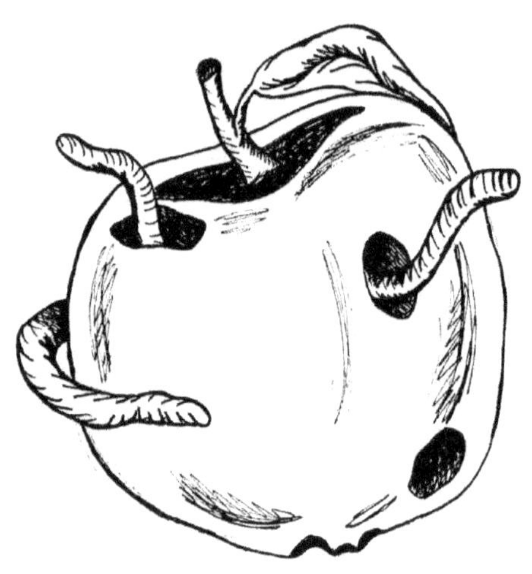

Chapter 3 Challenge

Choose one (Or all three if you're a daredevil!) to complete:

1)   Read back through the passages given from Mark and Matthew in this chapter. Beside each one write down a word or phrase that passage makes you think about Jesus.
Here are the passages: Mark 1:24-25, 3:11-12, 5:6-13, 9:25-26; Matthew 4:11, 4:23-24, 8:2-3, 8:13, 8:14-15, 8:16, 8:26, 9:2, 6-7, 9:20, 22, 9:18-19, 25, 9:27, 29-30, 9:32-33, 14:17-21, 14:25-27, 15:28, 15:30-31, 17:1-2, 17:26-27, 20:30, 34, 21:19, 28:5, 9.

2)   Read about the Armor of God
(Ephesians 6:10-17).
I suggest printing off the passage and marking it up.

3)   We often let worms into our lives because we don't feel we are worth fighting for ourselves. You are loved and lovable. You must love yourself because that is loving God. Write within the apple illustration what is loveable about you and names of the people who love you. Next, feel free to print off more apple illustrations for people in your life you want to encourage. Write in their apple things you love about them. Give them the apple illustration and tell them they are "loved and lovable." If you are doing this study with a group, I encourage you to do this for your study mates.

If you are doing this study with a small group, make time to discuss this challenge with them and encourage one another.

Chapter 3 Reflection

Challenge #3 Apple Illustration

Chapter 4
Soft Spots

Apples are a peculiar fruit. On the one hand they seem like such tough little critters. They can fall feet from a tree to bounce on the ground unscathed. They can be tossed through the air from one friend to another and remain intact upon impact. They can roll down hills, pump along in wagons, stroll in the bumpy shopping cart and take every hit like a man. They don't split, crack or bruise for just any old jostle. Apples are pretty hardcore like that.

But on the other hand, apples are a tender fruit. They are susceptible to all kinds of diseases and physiological disorders. Their beautiful appearance can easily be ruined by too much sun, too much shade, too much water, not enough water, one little insect, landing the wrong way one time, getting bumped too hard on another. Sometimes it just takes a smidge too much of one thing, or a smidge too little of another, and that tough little fruit is bound to die.

We humans are the same way. We are tough, but we are also so fragile. I love watching shows about what humans can survive - animal attacks, natural disasters, wars, famines, sickness. It is amazing what the human body can go through! We are tough little skeletons with mighty powerful little brains! And yet, we also have tender hearts that can be crushed by one word from a bully, and soft skin that can be scraped up from one trip. Sometimes you just never know what is going to be too little or too much that ends up breaking us.

One of the most common physiological disorders an apple gets is called "water core." I've always called them "soft spots." That is because before this book, I didn't do a lot of research on apples. I just grew up with them in my backyard and we farmers have a way of naming things so that is self-explanatory. A soft spot is exactly what it sounds like. You've probably bit into one in your lifetime. You repeatedly sink your teeth into a crunchy, hard surface of the apple. Over and over again you enjoy the crunch that comes with each bite. Then suddenly your teeth slide through the apple as if it were a banana. There is no chomp. It is as if you just took a spoonful of apple sauce. It takes you off guard. You look down at your apple and discover that the area is discolored. It is random and shocking - that bizarre soft spot in your apple.

I personally hate soft spots. They don't taste good. They're nearly flavor-less, but if they do have flavor, it definitely isn't appetizing. What I hate more than the taste is how they take me off guard. Most soft spots aren't visible on the outside of the apple. Some are, this is true. But most are under the surface, hiding their discoloration. There is no way to prepare for them. If you bite into one you have to decide there and then, with it in your mouth, if you are going to chew and swallow or make a scene at the family gathering and spit onto your grandmother's patio. Now you may be thinking I'm an awfully dramatic person. Soft spots aren't that bad, you may be thinking. To those two thoughts I really can't argue. I probably am a little dramatic and soft spots probably don't taste that awful and disappoint the average apple-eater all that much, but I really do love apples. When I eat them, I'm happy. So to me, the girl who believes with her whole heart that an apple a day can keep the doctor away, I HATE soft spots.

Here is where I start to turn this illustration around. My name is Kamra and I like apples. I also really like you. Who, Me? Yes, you - the reader of this book. I like you, not just because you obviously have really good taste in authors, but because God made you and loves you. I'm called to love you, aren't I? I'm even called to love my enemies - even you who might write a terrible review about this book or say this author is one apple who fell very far from the tree of knowledge. I will still love you because Jesus loves me and Jesus loves you. So you know what else that means? It means I hate your soft spots and Jesus does too.

Now, now. Before you chuck this book down the hallway, hear me out. Let me explain to you what these metaphorical soft spots could be in your life so you understand what it is I'm hating and claiming Jesus does too. Let me also preface this with making it perfectly clear that your soft spots are not who you are. To say I hate them, and Jesus does too, does not mean we hate you. Even if a soft spot is a part of you, it does not add to your identity. So, I can hate your soft spot and not hate you. After I explain what soft spots are, you'll probably agree you hate your soft spot too.

Too Much Water

Water core, i.e. soft spots, are areas within an apple's flesh that decay, moisten and often discolor, due to overexposure to water. Right off the bat you could read that and declare, How is water a bad thing?! I hear you, brother and / or sister! How could water possibly be bad for an apple? They need it to grow, obviously. But we must ask ourselves, can too much of a good thing ever be bad for you?

Cupcakes.

Oh, those sweet, fluffy, cute mini-cakes.

One cupcake with a pretty dollop of icing on top, nestled in a flowery foil, is the perfect dessert. It is portioned for you so you don't slice a giant piece of cake and overstuff. Everyone can grab one and not fight about who has the corner piece. Cupcakes are a celebration life-saver.

But eat ten of them and you're likely to sing a different song. Stuff your gullet with twenty cupcakes in one sitting and see how you feel afterward. Slide those savory dessert muffins down your throat a dozen at a time and see the fat appear on your thighs, the clogging happens in your arteries, and your blood sugar numbers go insane.

Are you catching my drift?

Too much of a good thing can be a bad thing.

Too much water for apples means a water core. Only so much can be absorbed and used appropriately to help the apple grow and flourish. Too much starts to build up. The cells of the apple start to drown. When they can't absorb anymore they start to break down and to soften. When you bite into a water core apple, you bite into a puddle of moist apple flesh. The water starts to rot the flesh, turning it from white to pink, then to brown. Eventually the water floods the entire apple, moving from the internal to destroy the outward appearance. Most often, an apple is disposed of before then, either eaten or discarded. It takes time. The destruction of the apple is gradual. I imagine it would be a painful death if apples could feel. It would be a slow drowning.

It ought to be obvious now how too much water is a bad thing for an apple. Now how about for you?

In the Bible water is a popular symbol. In the Old Testament it is used for ceremonial cleansing. People had to bathe in water to ritually purify themselves from sins, diseases and sorts of impurity. When they washed they were leaving those impurities and sins in the water.

That bathing pool became a place of holding death and sin. While you can't see sins floating on the top of water like green, gaseous bubbles, or turning the water from clean to brown, or laying on the tub floor like hippo dung, Israelites visualized their sins were floating there nonetheless. It was a pool of un-cleanliness after they had performed their ceremony there.

Water would continue to be a place that harbored bad things for the Israelites. They believed monsters lurked there, like the Leviathan. And they often drew the illustration of waters being like troubled times. Take a look at what David wrote in Psalm 69:1-2 & 15:

Deliver me, O God, for the water has reached my neck.
I sink into the deeps where there is no solid ground;
I am in deep water and the current overpowers me.
Don't let the current overpower me.
Don't let the deep swallow me up.
Don't let the pit devour me.

It was understood that to be overcome by water meant a person was being overtaken by difficult times. The prophet Isaiah put it like this:

When you go through deep waters, I will be with you.
When you go through rivers of difficulty, you will not drown.
43:2-3

God was needed in the water because it was in the water that they were experiencing feeling overwhelmed. Going through, and being in waters, was not a good thing back then.

For this reason, when God parted the Red Sea through Moses so that the Hebrews could escape the Egyptians, it was a remarkable miracle that would forever be told to all the Israelites. It meant more to them than an escape that day. God parting the waters so they could cross through on dry land was an incredible display of his power over all troubles and evil. From that point on whenever God wanted to remind his people who He was, He referred back to that miracle - that He was the God who parted the sea.

I am the Lord - who opened a way in the sea,
who makes a path in the mighty waters
(Isaiah 43:16)

A god who had power over waters was one who had power over every enemy, every trouble and every hardship. This was a god of ultimate power because water symbolized the ultimate evil.

God had power over waters.

Waters = bad

Therefore

God = good

In the New Testament, Jesus showed his divine power as God when he walked on the water and calmed the stormy seas. (See Matthew 8:23-27 & 14:22-33). Imagine being a disciple, one who believes there are monsters lurking beneath the surface and that troubled waters represent a troubled life, and you see Jesus walking over it at one point and at another telling it to shut up and it does. These miracles were not just statements of power; they were statements of the ultimate power. Jesus was God for only God could do that. The disciples who witnessed this were able to put their trust in Jesus. They had full confidence that he would bring them through anything that came their way. They would see that he could conquer death - that which water usually brought over them. He would trot right over death as if it were solid ground.

In Biblical times, too much water was not a good thing. Too much water meant they were drowning in troubles, being overtaken by sin and hardship. They did not want to be found in waters.

Today, there are still symbolic waters that are not good for you and I. There are things we let into our lives that damage us. In short, it is sin. S - I - N. These are the acts and thoughts that take us contrary to God's will. It is something that harms us. It makes us impure. It makes us less like God. It isn't good for us. It doesn't nurture holiness. It corrupts. It drowns. It takes over. It is invasive. Sin is deadly. Some of it is easy to spot and some of it isn't. Soft spots can look like many things and be many kinds of people, but they all have the same result -weakness, pain, death.

Humans have the amazing ability to leak water. Apples don't. When an apple absorbs too much water it turns into a physiological disorder they can't reverse. Once they have a soft spot, they are doomed to disintegrate. Not you and I. Do you know how we can release water when there is too much in us? We can cry.

Oh the wonderful bliss of being able to cry! Have you ever tried to hold in your tears before? Do you remember that giant lump that develops in your throat and it gets hard to breathe? It almost feels like you are actually drowning! You just can't get any air when your throat is clenched tight trying to keep down the waters. Have you busted? Like a water balloon that got too full - have you ever popped and exploded your waters? Do you recall the relief that came afterward?

Sometimes it feels so good to cry. Sometimes I cry for no particular reason. I could cry just because it has been a while since I had a good cry. There's something in me that feels relief when I can let out my tears. I absolutely hate trying to hold in my tears or not knowing if the space I'm in is a safe space to cry. If I feel I need to cry I just want to do it right then and there. I am that person that wants to cry unabashed, unashamed. Don't look at me. Look at me. I don't care. I'll cry during movies where a puppy finds his way home. I'll cry during commercials where a daughter calls her step-dad her father. I'll cry when I'm happy. I'll cry at good news. I'll cry from laughing too hard. I'll cry when I feel compassion. I'll cry when I feel sadness, and Lord knows I'll cry when I'm angry. In the words of Graham from The Holiday, "I'm a serious weeper."

But, crying does not always have to be watery tears. While I may be a literal puddle-maker, crying for you may be crying out verbally. Screaming, yelling, talking loudly, scribbling in your journal, whispering so intensely you sweat, moaning inaudibly, cussing a blue streak, curling your fingers into the mud of your yard, your fingernails against the bark of a tree, your fists upon the wall, your knees upon the cement... Crying out looks different for everyone. What matters is who you cry out to.

There's an untitled hymn many know as "Come to Jesus." One of the last verses say:
Sometimes the way is lonely and steep and filled with pain, so if your sky is dark and pours the rain
Cry to Jesus

There is a way to release our waters when there is too much in us. We cry out to the Jesus who can tread over them and tell them to be still with a whisper. Don't bottle it up and keep it inside. This will destroy you. Don't believe the lie that it will not cause you more damage if you keep it hidden and tucked away, or no one is there who will care to listen to it.

When an apple has water core damage it has a high risk of developing another physiology disorder: Bitter Pit. This disorder develops when water-soaked patches affect the flavor of the core. I bet a farmer named this disorder because it is very self-explanatory. When an apple gets this disorder the core tastes - you guessed it - bitter. The apple has spent so much time being flooded with water so it starts to taste differently all the way down to the core of it. Have you ever tasted a bitter fruit? It is harsh. It is tart. It makes you suck in your cheeks so you look like an infant going in for a kiss. It is a sharp flavor that makes you feel you just got stabbed with a sour sword.

People who let sin and troubles reside in their souls become bitter. People who stay put in the middle of life's storm just to prove a point and get a "woe is me" from those on the shore, are bitter. People who have hardships in their heart eventually taste like a hard lemon head. They're like cucumbers who decided to sit in the waters of vinegar and become mushy acidic pickles. They transform. They lose their good flavor.

Brothers and sisters, if we do not expel the sin from our lives, or reach out to the hand of Jesus when we are sinking into the gusty seas, we will become unbearable to be around. We will transform into exhausted, short-tempered and secret-keeping people. We will recluse from the community of believers. We will recoil from joy and praise. Eventually Christianity turns into just putting on a show, paying more attention to the flashing lights than the lyrics, and no one ever saying anything too right or too wrong, just medium warm and pleasant. Because when one person elects to live with soft spots, they want everyone to live with their soft spots too. This is what a bitter person does. They don't want solutions. They don't want harmony. They want to be miserable and everyone with them needs to be as well.

Is this who you want to be? Is this who we want Christians to be? Apples living with soft spots and accepting everyone with soft spots because then we are all soft-spotted apples? May it never be! We cannot become waterlogged people with bitter cores. We must hate soft spots for ourselves and for our neighbors. We must all acknowledge that we need Jesus lest we be transformed from the sweet-tasting apples we were meant to be, to pickles!

Many people acknowledge they don't want the buildup of sin and suffering in their lives and they try to release it through various means. Crying out is the only means in which humans can release water in its purest form. Unfortunately, many try to release their waters in other ways. For some, they take to cutting or harming themselves. Some people reach a point where they feel so full of pain (pain that can be caused by sin or hardships) they urge to feel a release. They physically cut, scratch, pick and rip away flesh until blood springs forth. In that moment, blood flowing may feel like the release of fluids they were needing. However, this release is fleeting. This type of release leaves scars and does not empty out the waters. No, it doesn't empty, just leaves them feeling emotionally empty because their mind has been refocused to the physical pain. Pouring out your own blood will not solve your water core damage. It will leave you feeling numb, emotionless, in pain, and scarred. You're releasing the wrong liquid.

Others turn to another form of physical release - sex. In this physical act there is also another kind of liquid that gets discharged from the body. Unfortunately, this release is short lived. It is all too temporary. After a few blissful seconds of forgetting where you are and all the troubled waters around you, it all comes crashing back onto the shore of reality the moment you slip your pants back on.

There are countless ways in which people try to release their pain or cope with the stormy waters of their life. Some turn to alcohol - another physical liquid that can temporarily make you forget your situation but only floods you more inside. Some turn to drugs. Some sleep around. Some just sleep. Some want to pretend there's nothing wrong. They mask up each and every day. Some add more lipstick, put on the fake smile, tighten the tie, pop the Xanax, eat the ice cream, play the video game, read the book, run the mile, lift the weights, binge the show, stay distracted, stay busy, stay asleep. Life goes by and the water within is never dealt with. These people will lie in their caskets a puddle of a person.

Don't let this be you. There is a method of release that works every time.

Confession

Crying out to Jesus is confessing your sin, your troubles, your soft spots. It is telling the Lord who hovered over the surfaces of the deep from the beginning of time that you know he knows what is inside you and saying you're sorry it is there. It is acknowledging out loud what you want to keep in the dark to the Light of the World. Confession frees your soul. It is the opening of the gate that lets out the floodwaters. It is what breaks the damn to your spiritual pool.

Confess your sins to one another and pray for one another so that you may be healed.
James 5:16

Your soft spot will never be healed if you don't acknowledge it and hand it over to the Healer. Your brothers and sisters in Christ ought to be there to hear you out and, therefore, keep you accountable to keeping out that sin, or out of those troubling areas. Now hear this, Christians: When someone has the courage to confess a soft spot, don't point at them and declare,

"Gross, they have a soft spot!" Take them into loving arms and do as James commanded: Pray for them. Pray healing over them. Lastly, accept the healing that comes from that beautiful lake-walking, ghost-looking, ship-sleeping, storm-shushing Jesus.

Confession of sins can happen over and over again. Heaven knows how often we sin. But there is one act of confession that every Christian ought to do once.

Baptism

This act of confession is a public one meant to show the world that we are dying to our soft spots and being renewed into the life of our Lord Jesus Christ. John the Baptist first started this practice. He called it the baptism of repentance. The Gospel of Matthew describes John baptizing people in the Jordan River as they confessed their sins (Matthew 3:4). Like the ceremonial cleansings in the Old Testament, this was a symbolic washing of inward filth. Jesus himself would go to John to be baptized. Though He had never committed a sin, Jesus wanted to publicly show the world that when you follow God you make a decision to die to sin and to live for Him.

That is what we are doing when we practice the sacrament of baptism. We are being buried with Christ through baptism into death when we are plunged under the water. When we raise up we are symbolically raising up with Christ just as He resurrected from the dead. We leave those sins and old ways behind us in those waters. We walk onto the shore and are dried up in the Son. We can stand on the bank and look back at those waters where a graveyard of sin, shame and troubles were laid to rest. We become conquerors through Christ. We are healed and restored through Jesus. Our soft spots are made new, taken away, purified from brown to white as if they were stains washed away in the water.

Do not continue to live with soft spots. Shouldn't we assume they'd be the easiest spots for a worm to enter in? Indeed! Confess, repent and be baptized. Go and sin no more. Be restored by Jesus. Live in the freedom that comes in the washing of the Holy Spirit. Amen.

Not Enough Water

Now we just spent a good bit of time talking about how too much water can kill an apple, but we have to acknowledge that all apples need some water to live! You don't have to grow up on a farm to know that an apple tree isn't going to produce well if it is a summer of drought. Nothing lives in a drought. Water is what brings life to our planet. It turns brown grass to green, dirt paths to streams. Water: It is a good thing.

"Excuse me, Kamra. Didn't you just give us this long explanation about how water is symbolic of bad things, like sin and hardship?" Yes, my sweet reader friend, I did. So the question becomes, how can something bad possibly be for the good? I'm glad you asked...

Suffering. Sin. Pain. You've gone through it. So have I. It is terrible stuff. It straight up sucks. While you were in those waters you were sure you were going to drown, that it was going to kill you. I've been there. I've sunk so low I lost sight of the surface above and felt as if my lungs were on fire from the sin and shame I was surrounded by. It is very difficult in those times, in those waters, to think it could ever be a good thing. All you want in that moment is to get out of them and never see them again. You don't just want to get to the surface or to the beach, you want to take a flight to the middle of Kansas and never see an ocean again. I get it.

But I have a testimony for you. Now that I am out of those waters, standing safely on the shore with my Savior, I can look out at the ocean I just crossed, got tossed back and forth in, sunk and drug across the floor like an anchor in, and say: I'm glad I went through it.

I've honestly always had a pretty easy life. I grew up in a Christian home. I have a wonderful mom and dad who love each other insanely. All of my family is Christians. We all went to the same country church most of my life. We prayed before every meal and every bedtime. We were in church every time the doors were opened. My parents were youth pastors for about twenty years so I got twenty years of teen-targeted retreats, concerts, conferences, lock-ins, mission trips, and more. Then I went to a private Christian college where I had chapel three times a week, wing church, small group, Sunday worship, Bible classes and theology professors to chill with. Instead of Resident Advisors we had Disciple Coordinators. Instead of spring break trips, we had mission trips. Then when I got out of college I married my high school sweetheart, a good Christian man who always respected and honored me and still does. He landed a great job that provides for us all that we need. We had a healthy baby girl and we bought a dream farm right down from his parents home. Not a lot of hardship there, if you didn't pick up on that.

But my waters came. I fell into sin. I got sidetracked from the Good Shepherd and wandered over to a rolling river like a stupid sheep. Before I knew it I was miles downstream kicking and baaing with all my might but the current was too strong and I was too weak. I got so exhausted from trying to get myself out with good works and pretending that I eventually gave up and decided to coast along. My wool got so soaked with the waters of this sin and hardship that I sank. Jesus, along with some of his disciples, had to come into the waters and fish me out. I flopped up on the shore gagging and spitting waters up from my lungs until eventually I could breathe again.

Now, when I stand on this shore with many of you, I can do three things. First, I can look at the sheep who have gotten caught in the same current I had and say, "I know what you mean. I know how you feel. I've been there." Second, I can say to the sheep who have never wandered into the rushing river, "I've been there and you don't want to go there. Learn from my mistakes. Stay close to the Good Shepherd. That water will kill you." And lastly, I can look at my Good Shepherd with water-washed eyes and say, "You're more good than I ever knew before. I didn't know you loved me like that until you rescued me despite me wandering away. If you'll do that for me, I know you will for everyone. Let me tell the world what you did for me."

That is the funny thing about suffering, sin, pain - you can learn from it all and you can be stronger afterward. He lets us go through this stuff so we can learn more about who he is, about who we are. Paul put it this way:

Suffering produces endurance, and endurance,
character, and character, hope.
Romans 5:3-4

That is what God does. He uses the bad for His good. He uses the darkness to contrast the light. I was totally destroyed and yet, God has made my weakness into strength. That is what he does. That is who he is. I am an instrument he gets to use to show his power, his love, his goodness and his plan for all of creation. I get to be a sun-dried lamb that tells God's story through my testimony. This is the gist of what I'd say: God flips everything upside down.

The symbol of water is transformed by Jesus in the New Testament. The ceremonial washing tubs that once symbolized a pool of unclean water filled with sin gets transformed to a pool of rebirth through baptism. The rivers of calamity in this life are promised to be rivers of everlasting life in paradise for those who believe in Jesus. God reverses the bad and makes it good.

Apples need water to grow just as humans need suffering to grow. Going through troubled waters makes us stronger. Crossing the ocean of hurt makes us understand compassion. It is the flood that makes us appreciate dry land, the seas for the shore. It is the rescue from the drowning that makes us appreciate the Rescuer, through liberation, the Liberator, through the saving, the Savior. We can rejoice in suffering for we know what and who it is for.

Does this mean we should allow sin into our life so that we can grow from it? Paul asked the same rhetorical question.

Shall we go on sinning so that grace may increase?
Romans 6:1

You know what his answer was?

Absolutely not!
Romans 6:2

It is not the act of sin that makes you more knowledgeable of God's saving power; it is Jesus helping you overcome sin that makes you aware. Being able to conquer sin is where the strength-building lies, not being able to live in and say you have the power to be saved. Strength is in the saving, not the sinning. Strength is in the Savior, not the sinner. Lord forgive us if we think the only way to know a greater Savior is to experience greater sin.

Jesus met a woman at a well. As she drew water for drinking, he told her to draw from him and she'd never thirst again (John 4:4-27). He was guaranteeing what he had was a permanent fix, a resolution. The water that flowed from Jesus was unlike any water she, or anyone, would ever experience. His water was different from what they all knew. His water wasn't symbolic of troubles. His water was symbolic of solution. That is because his water was flowing from a place of ultimate healing, perfect love, unending joy, unfathomable peace, complete faithfulness, incomparable holiness. His water was flowing out of Him, Jesus the God-made-flesh.

If anyone is thirsty, let him come to me,
and let the one who believes in me drink.
Just as the Scripture says,
"From within him will flow rivers of living water."
John 7:37-38

Here, Jesus throws in a quote from the Old Testament. Most likely, he was referencing Isaiah 58:11 which is a Messianic prophecy describing the one to come who would fulfill all God's people's needs like a water that would never fail. Isaiah would earlier describe that one day God's people would be able to draw water from the wells of salvation (Isaiah 12:3). Jesus also prophesied about this day - the day his people would be able to constantly draw upon the saving work of God. He promised his disciples the Father would send an advocate to be with them forever, the Holy Spirit, in his name (John 14:6, 26). He told them to wait for it - this water that would fall from heaven and baptize them in the Spirit (Acts 1:4-5). Then the day of Pentecost came.

The Spirit was poured out on them as if it had been liquidized and possible to swallow (Acts 2:1-4). It filled them up like hot coffee trickling down the throat and warming up their tummies. From that day forward it poured out of them onto all they encountered.

This Spirit is the same one that is freely given to all who believe in him. When you accept Jesus into your heart it is like being handed a cup of steaming herbal tea. You want it, just drink it. It warms you up so it is like fire that illuminates you from the inside out. But here's the coolest part: when you put the cup down, it is full again. You drink it, put it down. It is full again. Over and over again. It is a never-ending cup of hot Joe -s-u-s!

Feeling dry and like you can't possibly love one more single person that asks for your help today? Take a sip of Spirit.

Feel like you're running on empty as you take kids from place to place and still are expected to speak to them with grace and cook them dinner? Have a mug of Jesus.

Been trying to fill that void by having meaningless sex? Stick your straw into the Savior. It won't run out! It is a free, never-ending, life-time supply of his Holy Spirit!

You see, we-apples do need water. We need a little bit of suffering and just the right amount of Jesus. He knows how much we need. He is never in short supply. He's always in stock. He's right there on the shelf of your heart. He's nourishing you, refreshing you, giving you what you need to grow and sustain through each day. If you didn't have a little suffering, you wouldn't have much need for a Savior. Am I right?

I know it is hard to endure sometimes. Sometimes we feel like we're barely staying afloat and

other days we feel we've been wandering through a
desert. But take heart my swollen or shriveled friend:
"Behold, I am making all things new...
To the one who is thirsty
I will give water free of charge
from the spring of the water of life.
The one who conquers
will inherit this."
Revelation 21:5-7

The one who conquers. The one who endures
through the ocean of pain. The one who swims free from
the sea of sin. The one who keeps pressing on in the
wasteland. There is coming a day when you will reside
with the Water of Life himself, when you sit in the
presence of the Spirit, when you will thirst no more.
There will be no need to cry out then. Nothing to release.
We will be balanced, having all the water we need and
not an ounce we don't. Come, Lord Jesus, come.

Hi, my name is Kamra and I've had soft spots.
I've let sin soak into my life. I've resided in waters of
trouble for too long. At times, I've probably even been a
bitter pit. But I can say through it all, Jesus was there
and Jesus rescued. He used the bad to bring him glory.
He's shown me his goodness through the suffering. The
soft spots of my life were once easy entry ways for
worms to weasel in, but God has healed me and made
me stronger. I have cried out and I will continue anytime
the waters become too much. I know he will always hear
me and pull me out. He doesn't want me to get soft
spots. He just wants me to grow. He wants the same for
you.

Chapter 4 Reflection

1.   Are there sins you haven't let go of that are hurting you? Identify them, then work on surrendering those to the Lord.

2.   Have you gone through a season of suffering? In what ways were you strengthened through it? If you are currently in a season of hardship, ask for prayer, wisdom and endurance.

3.   Have you made a confession of faith and went through baptism? If so, describe it. If not, consider talking with someone about your faith and next steps.

God has a way of turning things around.

Label the illustration.

What are some examples of water, good and bad?

Chapter 4 Challenge

Choose one (Or all three if you want to get down to business!) to complete:

1)	Take into consideration what sins you may be letting erode you. Choose a close friend, or a trusted pastor or mentor to confess these sins to. Spill it all. Say out loud all that you are struggling with and need to let go. Ask that person to pray for you. You might consider making them an accountability partner. This is someone who will routinely check on you to see if you are staying out of those waters of sin. Be honest with them.

2)	Talk to someone about baptism. If you haven't been baptized, ask questions about it. If you have, ask someone else about their baptism experience. If they have been baptized, ask them what it meant to them. If they haven't, ask them if they have accepted Jesus as their Lord and Savior and if they would like to be baptized.

3)	Choose to fast from all other liquids except water for a period of time (48 hours, one week, one month). Each time you desire a different drink recite this verse:

"If anyone is thirsty, let him come to me."
John 7:37

If you are doing this study with a small group, make time to discuss this challenge with them and encourage one another.

Chapter 5
Bruised & Bitten

If you're like me, when you go to the store to buy apples (or any produce), you take your time examining each one before placing it into the bag for purchase. You want to make sure you get the best. You don't want an apple that has a rotten bottom. You don't want one that has a split down the side. Those apples will decay much faster than unblemished ones. So I pick the best-looking ones. Those are the ones we take home and display in the fruit bowl on the island. No one picks the bruised ones. Grocery store owners, and farmers with their market stands, know this. They don't put the ugly ones up front. Some don't even keep them on the shelves at all. Who knows how many fruits and veggies are tossed each year just because they have flaws.

The pressure is on the harvesters. The ones who pick and transport goods have the responsibility of making sure everything is treated with the best care to ensure less damages. I can only imagine the rage a farmer would feel to see an employee dropping and throwing around his apples instead of carefully placing them into the padded buckets. Carelessness would greatly increase the amount of bruises, cuts and scrapes an apple would get. A farmer could lose a lot of income with careless workers.

Imagine how enraged the farmer would be if he spotted his harvester taking a bite from the good-looking apples before tossing them into the bucket for distribution. As if he were test-tasting them for quality, the harvester nonchalantly bites out a chunk of flesh and then tosses the rest away. Outrageous!

There have been times I've dropped my bag of apples in the parking lot, or had them stepped on as my child climbs over the groceries into her car seat, or one simply slipped from my grip and smacked on the linoleum. I've even witnessed my sweet child take a bite out of an apple only to decide she didn't want it after all and puts it back into the fridge as if everyone should still be okay with eating it after she's slobbered all over it. During these times I shake my head, "Ruined!" Apples just don't taste the same when they're bruised and bitten.

It is probably blindingly obvious where I'm going with this, but here I go.

Raise your hand: Have you ever been bruised? Have you ever been dropped by someone and the pain shot through you like a smack to the linoleum floor? Has someone bumped into you, accidentally or intentionally, and left their mark? Do you have spots on your skin where someone bit into you with hate? Or do you have spots deep within that you desperately hope people don't see? You might believe they make you cheaper. You may believe they make you unwanted, unworthy. I had to stop typing for a moment because my hand was up in the air. Me. I have. I am. Bruised. Bitten.

Unlike water core spots, bruises are most often not self-inflicted. Bites certainly aren't. Bruises were given to you. Someone dropped you. They mistreated you. They didn't care for you properly. They neglected to hold you tightly. They were careless and reckless and you took the fall because of them. Maybe they bit into you. Sank their teeth in and left their mark. They took a chunk out of you without asking. You don't want bruises. You wouldn't choose them. They hurt and they're ugly.

The bruises and bites in our lives happen in a shocking instant. We call them traumas. A traumatic event can happen anytime, anywhere. It is an event that marks a turning point for us. It is at that moment we were impacted and pieces of our insides started to rot.

When an apple gets a bruise or bite the skin has been penetrated and a chemical reaction takes place between the outside oxygen and the cells of the apple's flesh. This chemical reaction begins to break down the cells, much like water core damage. The white flesh starts to rot, going brown. Limiting the amount of oxygen that gets to the wound (like refrigeration or wrapping the fruit) prolongs the apple's life, but bruising is irreversible.

For years people can try to hide a trauma. They feel the more attention they give it will only increase the damage. They believe the more oxygen they breathe into the trauma will only escalate the damaging effects. So they cover up. They metaphorically wrap themselves up. They use shopping, merchandise, friends and family, boyfriends and girlfriends, spouses, education, their job, their kids, their hobbies, their money, medications, alcohol, etc. We humans take anything we can get to wrap ourselves up. We believe layering in the newest fashions will cover our bruises. We believe sliding on the condom is like wrapping our bruises in rubber sheets. We think we can use hobbies like scrapbooking to paste over the cuts and scrapes of our hearts. We roll ourselves up in football as if it were saran wrap, and we cling to our professions as if they could disguise our wounds like a thick foil.

There's a funny thing about humans: we all have bruises and we all know that about each other, but we all do whatever we can in our earthly power to make it look like we don't have them. We'll do almost anything to make ourselves look like we've never been hurt. For some bizarre reason we all want to fool each other. We don't want the truth out there that we have traumas. But I think I know why we do it. We want to protect ourselves.

We want to put off this persona that we are strong, impenetrable, unbreakable. If others found out how we got bruised, they could know how to bruise us some more. So we pretend nothing has ever hurt us so people won't try to hurt us again.

We want people to look at us and say, "That girl is tough. Nothing gets under her skin." We want them to say, "He's solid. You can't get to him." We want to be able to say about that guy who just slept with us and didn't call back, "I don't care. He didn't hurt me." We want to be able to say, "She didn't mean anything to me. This won't impact me." We put ourselves in Ziploc baggies of lies so people might believe we don't have any bruises.

Some of us have bruises and bites we don't want anyone to ever know about so we hide. We crinkle ourselves into a brown paper sack and hope no one opens it up. We are afraid to talk about it, but possibly even more so, we are afraid to have them talk about it. We're afraid if we let someone peek into the brown paper bag, they'll start spreading the news of our bruises to the whole world. A gust of oxygen will sweep into the bag and rot us in an instant. No, it would be better if no one ever knew. So we hid in the darkened bedroom. We never speak of the past. Put a clip on the lip of the bag and never say a word.

This might work for an apple. For a while. But when an apple gets a bruise, there is no recovery, no bouncing back, no healing miracle spray, just the end of its life on the advance. For an apple. But for you, one little bruise, that gash of a trauma, does not have to be the end of you. Here's one area where what an apple doesn't need is actually exactly what a human does.

Oxygen

My five year old wants Band-Aids for all her cuts and scrapes. Sometimes she wants a band-aid even when there isn't a visible ouchy. Sometimes she wants one just because that is where she has a boo-boo. She finds comfort in having a Disney Princess band-aid over the spot where she got hurt. But sometimes I have to tell her to take off the band-aid. "Your boo-boo needs fresh air," I tell her. I remember my mother telling me the same thing when I was little. At some point all wounds need air to heal. They have to be exposed to the outside elements in order to cure. That gentle breeze comes along and eventually your cut starts to scab.

Our traumas are the same. Our bruises don't worsen with oxygen, they find healing. There is a great deal of relief that comes when we give breath to our pain. There's power to be felt when words can be put to our hurts.

Take this for example: Have you ever felt so passionately for someone that you can't keep in the words I love you any longer? Do you remember, or can you imagine, how relieving it was to finally let those words out? Or maybe this one: You've had a job that just poured anxiety and stress into your life to the point where you couldn't hold it in any longer - "I quit!" Like a bird that had its wings cramped inside a cage, did you feel like a free man after you walked out of that office? If not for these two examples, I'm sure you can think of a time where it felt breath-takingly wonderful, life-givingly blissful, to speak into existence the words you had been longing to let loose.

I know it may be hard to believe, but when you find the words and the lung capacity to talk about your bruise(s) and bite(s), I promise it will be freeing. It will be healing. You have to carefully choose who can be trusted with knowing such intimate details about you, but when you find that person, I guarantee it will relieve you. When you have the courage to crawl out of your crinkled brown paper sack and say to your sweet friend that which has been bothering you for so long, a burden will be lifted. I promise.

Just yesterday I had dinner with a woman I have met only once before for about two minutes. She approached me after a speaking engagement and wept with me - a complete stranger. She was going through a terrible time and wanted someone to just listen for a couple minutes. I did. Then we prayed. A couple days ago I got her contact information to follow up with this lady. I simply texted her that I was the stranger she had talked with and if she ever wanted to talk some more, I would listen again. The next day, we were having dinner.

I listened to this woman's story for a little over an hour over some Mexican food. As soon as we sat down I told her this dinner was all for her. She could talk as long as she wanted and shouldn't feel she is talking too much. I just wanted to hear her out. She spilled her guts while I dipped chips into salsa and nodded along. When she was done she took a deep breath as if she was relieved to have said it all. I didn't offer any advice, scold her for the sins she confessed, or give her my opinion on her current situation. I said, "Thanks for choosing me to share all that with." She graciously paid for my chimichanga and we went our separate ways.

I'll probably never know why this woman wanted to talk to me, of all people. I probably won't know to what extent that dinner may have been helpful. But apparently it was needed by her. She needed to give breath to her pain. She had so many internal bruises beneath that black Purdue shirt. She needed someone to listen. She didn't ask for my input. She didn't ask for Scripture or correction or a physician's referral. She just needed oxygen on her wounds.

What an amazing privilege it was to be picked to listen to her story. That stranger I met I then got to know so intimately in one dinner. She trusted me to see her bruises and I hope I didn't let her down. Sure, I didn't give her any amazing cures to her problems or tips on how to handle her situation, but I got to say, "I see you, and you are still beautiful." And what I said to her I say to you too: Bumps, bruises, scrapes, cuts, bites...you are still a child of God. You are not alone. I have them too. Let's talk about them over tacos. Let's heal together.

Now, to you who may be entrusted with learning about someone's traumas, I have a word. Listen. Nay, I have a paragraph. Shut up and listen to your friend, be they a new one or old. They have just opened up to you about something of great importance in their life. They are giving you the honor of looking upon something they traditionally keep hidden from the rest of the world. They are being vulnerable with you so be tender with them. Hold them with care, and hold your words with care! In that moment, when your friend pours out their heart and soul about a traumatic event in their past, you have the privilege of seeing them breathe into their wounds and you have power to breathe life back into your friend as well. Don't mess it up. Don't bug out your eyes and drop your jaw in gawking fashion at what they reveal. This is a life-altering moment. This is either a moment of freedom for your friend, or a chance to be condemned. Don't do the latter. Instead, take Paul's advice from Galatians 6:1-4:

> *Restore each person in a spirit of gentleness.*
> *Carry one another's burdens.*
> *Don't be impressed with yourself.*

Don't compare yourself to others.
If anyone thinks he is better than another
He deceives himself.

Stop pretending you don't have any bruises and bites. Everyone has been hurt at one point or another. Some people's wounds may be much bigger than yours. Some may be way more black and blue, but we all have them. Perhaps if people used social media to show their bruises instead of their wrapping papers, we'd all be more likely to stop judging each other and pretending we're spotless. It is really unhealthy to only view the perfected portions of people when all we see in ourselves is our discoloration. Let's be honest with each other. If you show me your wound, I'll show you mine. You know why? Because you need to know you're not alone.

A remarkable testimony is being able to point to a scar, say how you got it, and explain how it healed. I personally don't have as many cool survival stories as some of my family does. My brother can show you uneven layers of skin on his neck, chest and hands where he was burned as a child. My dad can show you his funny-looking thumb that was reattached after it was nearly pulled off in the corn picker. My scar isn't near as impressive, but I'll share it with you.

The tip of my index finger on my right hand is slightly misshapen. The tip of it was cut off in a deli slicer. In the summers between my college years I worked at a city meat market. One day a customer came in and wanted some ham, or turkey or bologna - I don't remember which. I placed the hunk of meat on the slicer and went to work. The chunk of meat kept getting smaller and smaller until I was shaving off the last few pieces of it. One of the last slices also happened to take off the top of my finger with it. I knew what had happened instantly. The pain shot up through my hand. Since I faint at the sight of blood, I quickly put my hand behind my back and finished weighing, bagging and ringing up the customer's order without looking at it. When I finished at the cash register, I turned to see a line of blood that was following me around the store. I knew the cut was bad. I took paper towels and rubber bands and wrapped my finger up, all while keeping it behind my back so I wouldn't see it. I finished my shift at work and headed home.

Hours after the slicing had happened, my parents got to take off the blood-soaked wrappings to examine my finger. As soon as the air hit the wound, I felt dizzy. My dad stuck it under the sink to wash off the blood and get a better look at the wound. When the water hit it, I fainted. When I came to, I was being taken to my parent's car. Before I got put in the seat I puked in the driveway. Then I was ready to go.

The doctor didn't have the tip of my finger to glue back on and there isn't enough skin to pull together on a finger to stitch up a wound. So I just had to put on some antibacterial ointment, wrap my finger in gauze and change up the bandages every six hours or so.

A few days after this emergency room visit I moved back to college. Every time I took the gauze off my finger it would pull at the wound where it had dried to the material. Each time it would bleed. Praise Jesus, my best friend and suite mate was a biology freak. She changed the bandages for me with glee.

Since my finger was wrapped with so much material, I drew a lot of attention. All of my friends thought the deli slicer story was hilarious and unbelievable. It got a lot of laughs, especially when they saw me try to type up papers or take notes in class. Eventually the wound healed, and now it is a great story.

I get to remember the wonderful man I worked with those summers at the market. He passed while I was in college from cancer. I have a voicemail saved on my phone from him. He sang "We are family!" Then he left me with these words, while fighting the battle for his life through cancer, "Miss you, kiddo. Keep looking up. God's looking after you." Andy MacDaniel was one of the greatest spiritual influences of my life in those college years. He spoke truth over me every day we worked together, grinding up burger, slicing up steaks. He made me laugh the way he would roll up bologna and put it in my shirt pocket as if they were pens and pencils. He'd slip one out randomly for a snack. He always told me if I turned sideways and stuck my tongue out I'd look like a zipper because I was so skinny. I could gut roll in laughter while bagging whole chickens. But I could also feel the warmth of the Holy Spirit as he spoke to me, even while stocking the freezer.

If I didn't have this scar on my finger I might not remember him so often and the words of life he breathed into me. Getting that cut was painful, not just that day, but for a couple weeks that followed as well. Yet, I wouldn't trade this scar for anything. It is fully healed now, but it still serves a beautiful purpose in my life.

Do you see where I might go with this? Your bruises, your cuts, your scrapes, your bites and traumas, all of them, are wounds that can be healed, and still afterward, serve a life-long purpose. But how do we get through the pain to the other side? How do we get to the place of healing and testimony?

Some bruises will heal through natural elements. Some just need exposure to fresh air. This may be in the form of talking it out, or being talked to. I highly recommend you see a counselor, therapist, psychiatrist, a pastor, or a trustworthy friend or family member who can give you good advice, listen to you and let healing be breathed over your wounds. With time and fresh air, scabs can develop, scars can take form, and bruises can fade.

Some traumas, however, need more than natural elements; they need supernatural. Luckily for us, Jesus is a breath of fresh air. His Word is a gust of truth. His Spirit is a wind of peace that surpasses all understanding. When it comes over someone they sit there in unbelief. It is unfathomably kind. It is miraculously healing.

Air is a symbol of the Holy Spirit in Scripture. In the beginning God breathed into Adam life (Genesis 2:7). That breath was spirit. It was what made Adam like God. It is what turned him from a dead thing into a walking, talking human with a soul. Throughout the rest of the Old Testament the Holy Spirit would sweep in and go through people that God needed to use. Judges, Kings, Prophets, they'd all be filled with the Holy Spirit like a breath. They'd say "The Spirit is upon me," as if it were a heavy wind temporarily blowing through them at that time. Unfortunately, the Holy Spirit was not able to reside within God's people permanently back then for a permanent substitute had not yet come to clean hearts. But praise God, he provided that permanent substitute through giving his only Son Jesus.

When the Messiah was here he prophesied about how the Holy Spirit would become a permanent resource, breathed into all God's people who would accept Him. Just as discussed in the previous chapter, Jesus told his disciples the Advocate, the Holy Spirit, would come to them if they waited for it. He, being the water of life, was going to leave part of himself, his Spirit, for them.

Do you know what the chemical compounds of water are? Hydrogen and Oxygen. H2O. Jesus, being the water of life, was leaving the Oxygen for his disciples! Like being composed of two parts, himself and Spirit, he elected to leave the Spirit for his people. Am I the only one who finds this entertaining?!

Hold onto your britches. It gets even better.

The Greek word for Spirit is πνεῦμα (pneuma). The first half of that word, *pneo*, is the Greek verb "to breathe" or "to blow." Thus, the Spirit is something that breathes or blows into people or things or around the universe. Specifically, it is the air that Jesus breathed into his disciples (John 20:22). It is the air that God breathed into Adam. It is the air that blew into the house on the day of Pentecost.

Suddenly a sound like a violent wind blowing
came from heaven and filled the entire house.
Acts 2:2

At that moment the disciples went out and started preaching, speaking in tongues to all the people around them. These people hadn't felt that gust of wind in the house. They obviously couldn't see the gust of wind either. They were perplexed and accused the disciples of being drunk. They couldn't understand the Spirit because they hadn't experienced it like the disciples had.

People don't know how to explain things they can't see. That is why another common translation for the Holy Spirit is the Holy Ghost. People can't see spirits. They can't see ghosts. They can't see the wind. But we sure can feel them. No one sees a breeze when it comes up off the ocean but they can feel the spray of water and note their hair move from their face when it blows. People can sense when a predator is watching them even before they see the glow of their eyes. People can feel an atmosphere thicken when "an elephant is in the room." There's the common expression, "You could cut the air with a knife, it was so thick." And if you've ever been in the presence of a spirit you can feel it. The hairs on your neck might stand up. Goosebumps could pop up on your arms. A certain emotion like fear, or peace, could override you. You don't see it, but you feel it there.

This is how the Holy Spirit is. He's constantly around though we may not always feel it or see it. He's giving life, constant and steady. He gives humans the ability to rise above just as air helps a bird fly, just as wind helps a leaf shake, just as oxygen helps a log float. He is the healing component to your cut, the Spirit for your slash.

The Holy Spirit can only do his work if you let him in. In other words, this hallowed wind can never clean your floor if you don't allow it in your house. Open your windows. Fling open the doors. Unbolt your trap and let him in so the bad can go out. He'll sweep your floor like no other wind could. While that counselor may be educated and spouting off all kinds of activities that could restore the damage done in your marriage, it can't compare to the deep cleaning the Holy Spirit can do. He isn't a Disney Princess Band-Aid. He doesn't mask bruises. You don't have to tolerate trauma. With a little bit of Jesus, you can be completely healed.

I asked it in the previous chapter and I'll ask it again here: Shouldn't we assume these spots (our soft spots, bruises and bites) are the easiest entry ways for worms? When an apple is dropped and bruised, it often busts open at the skin. When bitten into, a gaping wound is left visible. A worm could slide right in. If left untreated, these spaces are wide open doors for the Enemy and his wormy army. We must accept heeling to our peeling.

On the natural side, it is easy to see. My finger doesn't look the same, but it is all better. I'm typing like mad man over here! My dad never thought he'd play the guitar again, but his thumb can hold those chords better than ever. My brother had hundreds of staples holding in someone else's skin grafts onto his bald and scalded bones, but now he's staple-free and so hairy you can't even see his scars!

On the spiritual side, we each have been healed as well. I won't speak on behalf of my brother and father, but I was traumatized in childhood, banged and beaten up in marriage, bullied and bruised in previous careers, bitten in unhealthy relationships, but I was healed. Guess what, you can't see those scars and how they transformed me, but I am different because of them. They changed the way I look. Innocence may have been cut from me. Words may have shot through me like bullets leaving holes in my heart. But the Holy Spirit stitched me back together with affirmations of truth, filled me back up with joy, hope, peace and love. Something may have been sliced off but I grew more compassion in its place. Pain may have lasted for a while but it has been fixed with assurance of faith.

Our traumas and bruises won't go unnoticed by God. He has a knack for taking the bad and making it into something good. Those tears won't be wasted. God will grow something beautiful from them. Your black and blue bruises, your scars, they all make one beautiful canvas to the Lord. He isn't the type to discard an apple for one little blemish. He doesn't point at you and say, "Hide behind the Christians who look better. Sit in the back row. Stay backstage." I guarantee he says,

"There's my beautiful son. I will hand out justice to the one who bruised and bit you. In the meantime, let me hold you. I'll restore you, and boy, you will have one heck of a testimony!"

This leads me to give a word of caution for you bruise-makers and biters. To you who have been careless with my fellow apple-sisters and brothers: you will pay for that. Unless, of course, you repent and are sorry for what you did. God forgives you. But still! Let this be a lesson to all of us about the importance of taking care of our fellow neighbors. We can easily damage one another. Sometimes dropping someone is accidental. Sometimes you didn't mean for that person to get hurt. I get it. I've done that. But other times, you did. You meant to throw that word at them that would pierce their heart. You purposely brought up the past so you could see them crumble. You bit them just to taste them. You talked down to them so they'd feel smaller. You poked fun at them so you'd feel bigger. Whatever it was, you have to recognize that it could have caused greater trauma than you know.

If you want a great example of what I'm talking about watch the movie *Benchwarmers*. A grown man has to face a fellow classmate he once bullied. That victim was badly traumatized by him. It was painful to see how he had coped with the bullying over the years. It was eye-opening for the bully to realize what his words and actions had done to him. Each of these men found healing by the end of the movie. The bully found it by saying out loud he was sorry. He asked for forgiveness. The victim was healed by accepting that apology and saying in return, "You're forgiven." That little bit of oxygen healed a lifetime of pain both people had been carrying, one from guilt and one from fear and hatred.

To you wound-makers, stop it. "Vengeance is mine," says the Lord (Deuteronomy 32:35). Justice will be dished out to you if you do not stop it. God loves his children and he hates when they are hurt. Don't be on my Dad's bad side. Fix what you've wounded and try with all your might to never hurt again.

Now, to those I have hurt, I am sorry. If I've had the chance to apologize to you in person, I hope I've taken it. If I haven't, I hope you can read this and know that I'm sorry. I hate the idea of knowing I may have caused someone an injury. Please accept my apology.

Hi, my name is Kamra. I have bruised people and I'm sorry about it. I too have been bruised and bitten. I have scars on my skin from wounds Christ has healed me from, but I still have a few I'm watching Him heal. He will do it in his time. But I'm still a pretty apple. I'm still worth the purchase. I know I am because he showed me by taking his own scars and bruises. I get to be more like him now, with these hurts and boo-boos. I get to be taken care of by the best father and physician in the world. So I won't hide in my brown paper sack. I'll still be a vulnerable little fruit, so soft and damageable. But if that helps me be more like Jesus, bring it on.

Compression

Sometimes we know when we've hurt someone. We know because we intentionally dropped them. We meant to hurt them. We wanted to see them bust. Sometimes, however, we hurt people without knowing it. You see there are two main ways an apple gets a bruise. One, through blunt force, like what we just talked about in the previous section. Two, through compression. This second way is often unintentional, just a natural coincidence to living with other apples. Let me explain it.

Apples can be damaged when they have too much weight pressing down on them. Apples start to collapse from the weight of other apples laying on top of them. If you see a bundle of apples in a bag or stored in a drawer in the fridge you may notice the ones on the bottom are the most bruised. They have been smashed by those on top. They are being pressed into the bottom of the hard refrigerator floor and they're bruising from it, or they're being smashed from up above by heavy apples casually laying on top of them.

If you've ever had a heavy person sit on you, you know what I'm talking about. I can see Kevin Malone from the TV series *The Office* sitting on Michael Scott's lap when he dressed up as Santa. Michael Scott moaned in pain as the overweight man plopped down on him like a little child. Hilarious! But for Michael Scott, he was in pain. He felt the full weight of Kevin and it caused his legs pain.

Likewise, there are people in our lives who decide to sit on our laps that are heavy. People stack on top of us or are shoved into the same bag we are that are heavily burdened. There's all kinds of heavy people. Some carry a lot of emotional weight. They are spiritually down trodden and collapse upon others in a heap of deep tears. Some people are heavy because they're intentionally holding onto things they should have let go of. Some are lugging around twenty extra pounds of baggage from the past. Everywhere they go and every person they encounter has to deal with a person who is packing around an entire suitcase of grudges. Some keep words people said long ago in their pockets like boulders. Some tuck bowling balls of anxiety and worry in their hoodies as if it was something they must carry with them. Heavy apples. They're everywhere, I tell you.

Everyone will be heavy at some point. It is inevitable. We will be burdened down by a death in the family, a loss of a job, a breakup, a bad report, a stressful situation. We all will have burdens at one point or another and we will be heavy. That is okay. We all come with baggage and weight.

The beautiful thing about being stuffed into a bag with other apples is that means there are other apples to help carry our weight. The great thing about community and not being the only human to exist on this planet, is that we can help lift each other up when we are feeling too heavy to stand on our own. Paul implored the Galatians to support one another. "Carry one another's burdens," he said (6:2). It is imperative that we sustain each other. We need each other. Adam needed Eve. I need my parents and husband. I need my church family. I need my best friends. My daughter needs me. We all rely on each other.

If right now you are thinking you don't need anyone, you're wrong. You need farmers who grow your food. You need doctors who give you care. You need power plant workers who provide you electricity. You need waitresses who bring you cheeseburgers. I can go on and on. We need each other. The world would be really difficult to run if you were alone.

Unfortunately, we have some apples who don't want to help carry other people's weight. We have people who want to lay around and smash others underneath them. Don't worry, I'm not about to get on a welfare kick and take a political turn. I don't speak that language. What I'm saying is there are people who elect to be heavy all the time, needing people to lift them up, and never will they lift a finger for others or see the damage they're putting on those they're relying on.

People can be oblivious to how much weight they've put on another person. Kevin Malone, in his goofy innocence, sat upon his boss' lap thinking for minutes about what gift he should ask for. All the while, Michael Scott held his breath and pleaded for him to hurry up. Some people lack self-awareness. They are so blinded by their own problems, so deep in their world of stress, they forget other people have problems too. They take and take and it doesn't occur to them they ought to give back.

These people can be hard to deal with. If you have a heavy apple in your life right now, you know what I'm talking about. You see that person coming and you think, "Get ready to pour yourself out for this person. Give them your energy, your money, your advice, your listening ears, and don't expect anything back. Don't expect a thank you. Don't expect them to actually take your advice, or even give you a second to share it." You brace yourself when this heavy apple comes around.

Unfortunately, we will always have these kinds of apples. We will always have people who choose to be selfish, not caring if they're hurting others so long as they stay toward the top of the apple bag. We could call them out. We could try to make them more self-aware, but there's a good chance these apples won't change. They've become reliant so much so that they probably won't ever know how to carry someone else's burdens. They are the type of people who won't offer to carry a load because they have too much of their own weight to deal with. It's sad, but this is reality.

The best chance we have for these types of apples to change is 1) they see the bruises they are making on others, or 2) they experience the joy of carrying someone else's burdens and want to change. For those of us who may have a heavy apple currently on our lap, we can choose how to move forward. 1) We can try to show them the bruise they are leaving on us by remaining heavy and unwilling to move on or change. 2) We can push them off and not allow them back onto our laps. 3) We can let them stay, never say how they're crushing us, and we will be damaged by them. None of these options are necessarily easy but I hope you make a healthy choice for yourself.

On the flip side, we apples need to stay aware of our weight. No, no. Don't pull out the scale and hide your candy bar right now. I'm not talking about a fat to muscle ratio. I'm talking about keeping your mental and spiritual well-being in check. I'm talking about making sure we are casting our cares upon the Lord. I'm talking about making sure we are frequenting the Savior who graciously takes our burdens and makes us light again. When was the last time you took your worries to Jesus instead of only to your mother? When was the last time you prayed to your Father in heaven instead of picketing your earthly dad's pockets?

Now don't hate me. God gave you these people to help you, yes! But he also gave HIMSELF so you could have him as a resource. He wants to be the one you go to for help. He wants to hear your worries. He wants to know what is troubling you. He cares about it. Even the small things. Someone called you a loser? Jesus wants to hear you vent about that. You only have $10 in your bank account? God wants to provide for you in miraculous ways if you'd ask him. Afraid of starting your new job? Stressed out about your son's life choices? Anxious about tomorrow? He wants you to come to him!

Come to me, all you who are weary and burdened, and I will give you rest.

In Jesus we find peace. In his presence we become weightless. WEIGHTLESS. That is why Paul could say "where the Spirit of the Lord is there is freedom" (2 Corinthians 3:17). We are unchained from sin and shame, guilt and our pasts, bruises and traumas. We are a people who can be released from these bondages. We are transformers. We are caterpillars who become butterflies. We no longer crawl. We fly. His Spirit does that to us.

So I ask, do you know why someone might choose you to confide all their bruises in and confess their sins and share their life story with? It could be because they feel the presence of the Lord when they are with you. They feel that liberating Spirit! There is peace in your companionship. People feel comfort in the presence of Jesus. They know when they are in good company. If you have the Spirit within you, they can sense that, like a gentle wind blowing into their life.

It sounds like a lot, doesn't it? To have to carry someone's burdens, to have to care about other people and love them. It's exhausting! It would be so much easier to just not care. I hear you.

Here's the good news: When you have Jesus in you he's the one that gets to take these people's burdens that you are encountering and carrying. People who don't have Jesus just have to take other people's weight upon their shoulders and have nowhere to put it. Not you and I. We get to carry someone's burdens to the

Savior. We don't have to carry their load forever. We get to take it to Jesus. We can't force them to do that, but if they entrust us with something, we don't have to let it weigh us down. We give it to Jesus and we can encourage them to do the same.

I didn't have answers for that woman who wanted to have dinner with me yesterday. She didn't need more to-do's heaped onto her burrito anyway. Instead, we took it all to the Lord. We prayed. And I'll continue to pray for that lady. I'll pray that she takes her cares to the Lord and leaves them at his feet. I've taken the heavy information she gave me and I've given it to Jesus. He knows what to do with it. He can fix it. I can't. How freeing is that? We don't have to have the answers. We don't have to give the best advice. We turn to Jesus who sits beside us and says, "What do you think? You got this? You know tomorrow and the next day and the day after that? You know all these people and all these places and all our situations? Great, then I trust you to deal with it."

That is the great thing about having Jesus. When you have him, you don't have to worry. So then, I ask you:

Why do you worry saying,
"What will we eat?" or
"What will we drink?" or
"What will we wear?"
For those who don't have God run after these things,
but your Heavenly Father knows that you need them.
So don't worry about tomorrow...
Matthew 6:31-31, 34

When we elect to stay heavy, stay stressed and our minds crowded with worry, we are choosing to turn our face from Jesus. There's a verse I left out of that passage above. Verse 33 is the answer to how we stop worrying. It says, "Above all this, run after his kingdom and righteousness, and all those questions - what to eat, drink and wear - will be taken care of." Essentially, keep your eyes on Jesus and everything else will fall into place. Helen H. Lemmel wrote,

> *O soul are you weary and troubled*
> *No light in the darkness you see*
> *There's light for a look at the Savior*
> *And life more abundant and free*
> *Turn your eyes upon Jesus*
> *Look full in his wonderful face*
> *And the things of earth will grow strangely dim*
> *In the light of his glory and grace*

Looking to Jesus is so important. When our eyes are set on him we can throw off the sin that so easily entangles us and run! (Hebrews 12:1-3)

If you are continuously soaking yourself in his presence, you find the strength to carry other people's burdens because in his presence you are relieved of your own.

I once had a friend say to me, "How do you have so much to pour into me?" I was able to tell her, "Because God pours so much into me." I was able to say that because I was practicing being in God's presence every day. It became a priority for him to pour into me. I needed him because I was finding more and more people around me who needed him. If I was going to give him to all these people, I was going to need a lot more of him for myself.

In 2023 I couldn't have done that. In 2023 I probably hurt a lot of people because I was so heavy. I was full of stress and anxiety and sin. I was self-absorbed. I was weighed down with shame and guilt. I bet I was compressing against people left and right. I wasn't helpful in 2023. I was laying on the refrigerator shelf of life on top of coworkers, family and friends saying, "I can't move. I'm just going to lay here on top of you. Please deal with it." Of course I didn't know that at the time. I didn't know I was compressing people. I honestly felt more alone than I ever had. But now that my burdens have been lifted unto the Lord I see how heavy I must have felt in other people's presence. For this, I have a lot of regrets. I feel sorry for how I was lazy and lax in my faith. I missed out on a lot of opportunities to help other people with their burdens last year because I was too distracted by my own. Every day I didn't cast my cares upon the Lord was a wasted one. Learn from me. Please absorb these words. Don't remain heavy. Freedom is waiting for you with arms open wide and ears ready for listening. Jesus is there. Go to him and drop the weight at his feet. He can handle it. He's super strong.

Hi, my name is Kamra and I can be a heavy apple. I can get really loaded with stress and anxiety. I can lean on people far too long and ask way too much. For those I've bruised by doing this, I'm sorry. But I'm also learning how to take my weight to Jesus and drop the pounds. I'm freeing myself up for more people like you, to help carry your burdens. I'm happy to do it, and I'm happy to help you take your burdens to Jesus too. I can't remove them, but he can.

Chapter 5 Reflection

1.   Have you ever been physically bruised or injured and may have a scar to prove it? Share stories and reflect on how the healing came about.
Turn now to the spiritual bruises and bites you may have. How did you get them and how have you healed?
2.   What are common ways you see people trying to hide their bruises today?
3.   What are things that commonly weigh people down in our society or generation?

Let oxygen get to your wounds so you may heal and be set free.

Label the illustration.

Give examples of what bruises or bites (traumas and painful circumstances) may be. Identify your own.

Chapter 5 Challenge

Choose one (Or all three if you're a spicy Christian!) to complete:

1)   Apples get bruised two primary ways - blunt force or compression.
Take stock of yourself. Have you been bruised or bitten? Give oxygen to your wound by talking about it or writing it all down.
If you choose to talk about it, choose a friend or trustworthy mentor that will listen and pray for you.
If you write it down, ask God to help you heal and deal with your bruises. Hand the paper over to him by doing one of the following. One, fold the paper up and write "Healed" on top. Place it in your Bible or journal. Two, discard the paper by throwing it in the trash, in a body of water, or by burning it. When you release that paper, know what you wrote down is out of your control and in God's.

2)   Time for self-reflection.
Are you feeling weighed down or heavy?
 Make a list of everything you are worried about. Write down all that you feel you are carrying (financial obligations, parents, school work, etc.).
Look over this list and cross off everything that is in regards to the future or the past. Next, cross off everything that you can't control. Lastly, cross off everything that is known by God.
Take a look at your paper now. Everything should be crossed off. Do this as many times as needed throughout the week when you feel burdened or overwhelmed.

3)	Grudges are bruises we don't want to let heal. If you have unforgiveness toward someone, now is the time to give it.
Go to the person you have built up a wall against and grant them forgiveness. You are not granting them permission or access to hurt you, but you are freeing yourself up from the anger and hostility you have kept inside.
If you cannot physically go to them, write them a letter or send them an email.
If you can no longer connect with them, write it all out in formatting of your choosing and imagine giving it to them. Say everything you fear you couldn't say in person. Then be free from the anger that is tied with them. It is time to let it go.

If you are doing this study with a small group, make time to discuss this challenge with them and encourage one another.

Chapter 6
Tough Skin

We just learned in chapter five that when an apple's skin is broken, bruises set in and they spread every second outside elements, like oxygen, get inside them. In chapter four we learned the more water an apple absorbs through their skin creates soft spots on their insides. It is all coming together to show us just how important the skin of an apple really is. It is the first line of defense. It is the protective barrier. The skin is like a shield.

I'm sure you've heard the expression, "You need to have tough skin." I can't tell you how many times I've been told that. It is commonly said to those who are sensitive.

Hi, my name is Kamra and my "skin" is about as thick as tissue paper. Say one wrong word to me and I'm likely to burst into tears. Look at me wrong and I'll cry when I get home. Don't say anything. Don't even be in my presence. But if I hear I hurt your feelings or you were talking negatively about me . . . you guessed it, I'll cry my eyes out.

People have told me countless times that I need to toughen up. I need to get calloused. I need to get hard. I need to stop caring so much about what people think of me. Care less. Cry less. Etc. Etc. To these people I need to make a point perfectly clear: There is a fine line between having tough skin and having a hard inside.

People make the mistake of believing that to have tough skin means you become a rock from the inside out. The solutions to problems become a heart-hardening one, instead of a protective measure. Take this example:

Problem: You cry after each meeting with your supervisor because of the hateful tone they use towards you.
Solution: Stop caring about your supervisor.

Do you see how this solution isn't a protective measure, but a heart change? You are adjusting your identity, your God-given ability to love others (even your enemies) for a hard interior. Note the difference:

Problem: You cry after each meeting with your supervisor because of the hateful tone they use towards you.
Solution: Care enough about your supervisor to ask why they speak in a hurtful tone. Seek conversation with them that may get to their heart and help them better understand yours as well.

The response of a person who has tough skin according to the world will get hard on the inside and choose to stop caring. Those who have tough skin like Jesus are electing to put on more compassion.

When I look at Jesus in the Gospels I see a man who definitely had to have tough skin. He was hated by so many. He was even betrayed, stabbed in the back, by one of his best friends. He had the amazing ability to be able to stand up to the Pharisees when they claimed he was demon-possessed, a false teacher, and a nobody from Nazareth. I'm sure he had to listen to bullies say his mom was a slut and he was a bastard child. I'm sure he got mean looks when he slept on the side of the road and in the woods. Yet, through it all, he was able to cling to his identity and uphold his true character. He was able

to be the most compassionate, forgiving, loving, and giving man to ever walk the earth. How did he do it? How was he able to have tough skin, keep doing what he was meant to do, and still remain so soft on the inside, doing everything with overwhelming grace?
I'll tell you how.

Jesus lived fully suited everyday in spiritual armor.

The tough skin of Jesus was not a fake facade. He was not pretending to care less about people than they cared about him. He didn't need to appear stoic. He wasn't one to hide his feelings about a person or a subject. Over and over again he was overwhelmed with compassion. He was moved into action. He reacted. He felt. He cared.

When his best friend, Lazarus died, he wept. When he saw a leper, he reached out and touched him. When he heard a mother wailing, he raised her dead son to life. When he looked upon the Centurion, his heart went out and the servant was healed. When he saw the temple of his Father had become a marketplace, he fashioned a whip and screamed. When he encountered the adulterous woman, he knelt down in the dirt. The estranged woman at the well - he befriended. The soldier who chained him, he healed his ear. The mockers at the feet of his cross, he asked his Father to forgive.

Jesus wasn't an impenetrable stone. He was just tough enough to be smacked in the cheek and turn the other one in response. He was always doing the opposite of our fleshly reaction.
When a cloak was asked for, he didn't say, "Get your own." He gave the one off his back and a spare.
When the world said, "Be tougher," he said, "Be kinder."

The world said, "Richer," while he said, "Blessed are the poor in spirit."
His disciples said, "Fight." He said, "Blessed are the peacemakers."
Your dad said, "Suck in your lip. Be a man." Jesus said, "Blessed are those who mourn."
Your coworker said, "Don't let them walk all over you." Jesus said, "Blessed are the merciful." Society said, "You're a Jesus-freak. You don't fit in. You need to bend. You are peculiar and odd. You will lose your job. You'll lose your friends. . ." Jesus said, "Rejoice and be glad! Blessed are you who are persecuted."

What God has in mind is usually the opposite of what we have. So when we are hearing we need to have tough skin, we need to put off the physical mind. We need to think spiritually. Most of the things that cut to the heart of us aren't physical anyway. They are words. They are glares. They are rumors. It is gossip. It is all invisible arrows. So we don't need a vocabulary of come-backs. We don't need bigger biceps. We don't need forgetful minds or harder hearts. We need an invisible shield. We need a protective bubble that blocks the unseeable. We need what Jesus had. We need the armor of God.

When the early church was being established, Paul exhorted the people of Ephesus to put on this armor. His whole letter of Ephesians is about how to live Christ-like. He explains they need to be aware of who Christ is. He inserts a couple prayers throughout, prayers asking God to show them the full measure of his love. He explains they have to live in unity, live in holiness, live in love, in light, in wisdom and live spiritually aware and armored. So if we want to live like Christ, we probably should look at these pieces of advice in a bit more detail.

1. Live in Unity

The people of Ephesus weren't Jews. At least not most of them. They were Gentiles, Pagans. They were people who worshiped Greek gods. This city would become one of the seven wonders of the ancient world because of their massive temple housing the statue of Artemis - the fertility goddess. You can only imagine the types of offerings made, the symbols and carvings that had to be displayed in and on this temple. These were a people deeply enslaved to the sin of sexual immorality, among other impurities.

BUT Jesus came. He gave all people the ability to come to God through him. He made a way for all people to be saved, Jew or Gentile, Ephesians or Israelites. This is the main point of Paul's letter. He reminds them of their new identity. They are no longer worshippers of Artemis. They are no longer outcasts. They aren't people who need to be circumcised in order to fit in. They are grafted into the family of God. They are sons and daughters, children of the promise. In other words, they are no longer alone. They have been brought near by the blood of Christ into a family, called the Church.

In order for them to stay rooted in this identity, it was imperative they stay congregated. When you're all alone, it is easy to lose sight of who you are. When you are a part of a team, you have a common purpose. You have a mission. You have goals and a significant part to play on your team for corporate success. When you're a part of a team, you share a name. The Kansas City Chiefs. The Atlanta Braves. Mount Pleasant Baptist Church. Christians.

When you become a part of a team you take on their identity. You wear their colors. You slap their logo onto your bumper. You parade around in matching shirts. You have an identity and when you're with your teammates, you can't forget it. It is all you see. It is what you talk about. But when you're alone, you forget. You can put on any old shirt. You can change your colors as many times a day as you like. You can talk about anything, watch anything, say anything, do anything. No one is there to keep you accountable to your team's pride. Spend enough time alone and you'll eventually forget it all. You'll forget the colors, the names of the other teammates, what position you held, where you were going and why you were going there. Unless you join another team, you become aimless. Your identity is fluid, un-solidified, un-rooted.

Paul encourages the Ephesians that if they don't want to lose sight of their new identity in Christ, they have to make it a practice to live in unity. In order to grow up into Christ they must make every effort to keep a bond of peace. The Ephesians and the Jews, the Hoosiers and the Cheese Heads, the Baptist and the Methodists . . . When we play for Team Jesus, we have to live in unity. Satan loves dissensions. He loves factions. He loves separation. He loves divorce. He loves to get you alone. You're easier to kill that way.

Your skin is toughest when you are
in community.

2. Live in Holiness

God is the most holy being to ever exist. He defines holy. He has angels in heaven that surround him with a continuous chant, "Holy, holy, holy is the Lord God almighty." There's no better way to describe him - Holy. So if we want to be like Christ, the unblemished, perfectly flawless, tough-skinned Jesus, we have to live in holiness.

How, Kamra? How do I live a holy life? There's a whole lot to that question, so let me just highlight the three don'ts Paul says in 4:17-32.

1) Don't live as Gentiles do.

Gentiles is a general biblical term for people who were not of the family of God. They traditionally were not of Jewish descent. They usually practiced pagan ways, like worshiping other gods instead of one. Paul describes them as being "futile in their thinking." That means most of what occupied their minds was useless garbage. They spent their days living aimlessly. They had no direction. They were people who didn't have a team. They were living for themselves; therefore, they lived to pleasure their flesh. They chose to act in all kinds of selfish ways: sexual immorality, impurity, depravity, idolatry, sorcery, in hostility, envying, murdering, getting drunk, cussing and fighting. Because of these choices, they became alienated from God and others. They became hardened in their hearts and they became calloused. They went too far when it came to having "tough skin." They became angry, bitter and ugly.

Apples with too tough of skin do the same thing. There's a couple popular skin disorders apples can get: Russet and Scarf Skin. Both are pretty similar in appearance and both can come about from the same environmental stressors. While there's a good list of biological factors that can cause these disorders, the most common is cold temperatures.

Russet and Scarf Skin are diseases that affect the skin of an apple. Scarf skin, most likely named by a good ol' farm boy, is pretty self-descriptive. It is a layering on the skin that is contrary to the silky smooth surface it is supposed to have. If you were to rub your finger along the flesh it would feel bumpy like a wad of yarn bubbling at the surface. Like a scarf, it can often wrap around the apple in circles. These are commonly known as frost or freeze rounds.

If you live in Indiana you are all too aware of the atmospheric shifts our climate goes through. It could be a sunny, calm, 70 degree day on Monday but on Tuesday it could be hurricane-like winds and plunging to the 20's. We've all probably had to go out in March and throw sheets over the sprouts because a late frost has decided to call our names. Welcome to the Midwest.

These abrupt temperature shifts can damage the skin of an apple. If their skin isn't fully mature, tough - in other words, then it will callous and change colors. The only assurance an apple has at not getting damaged by a freak snowstorm in midsummer is to be ripe. When an apple has fully matured, the skin is tough, fitted, ready to fall from the branch and not split on the ground.

How does an apple ripen?
It is such an easy question.
You know the answer.
Through the SUNLIGHT!

If I picked an apple from our trees as I was growing up, instead of picking one up from the ground where they're clearly ready for eating, I could notice where the sun had hit the apple and where it didn't. The side of the apple that faced inward, hidden in the shade of a branch or leaves, was not as red as the outside that had full sun. The shaded spaces of the apple's skin were pink, green, even white. You can look at an apple and tell if it is ripe. You can tell if it has been in the sunlight.

Now let's flip this back on us apple-humans.

When we Christians are fully mature we should also be ready to face sudden atmospheric shifts, falls, drops, i.e. the difficulties life can un-expectantly throw at us. Mature Christians ought to be able stay shiny smooth when times are blistering freezing, because they've been ripened in their time sitting with the Son. They are constant all the way around. They are solid in color, in appearance, at each angle you look at them.

- In celebration - they rejoice.
- In the hospital - they rejoice.
- In a gorgeous mansion - they delight.
- In the rubble of a house fire - delighting.
- While getting applauded - they smile.
- While getting ridiculed for Christ's sake - smile.
- In sickness and in health - they worship.
- In a relationship or alone - praising.
- On the mountaintop or in the valley - they say, "God is good. All the time."

A ripe Christian doesn't have discrepancies when they are examined. They should allow Christ to shine upon them in all areas. They don't keep a place hidden from the Lord. They trust him with their whole being. They see where there is a weak spot, a pink underbelly, and they expose it to Jesus. "Ripe and mature in this area," they pray, "Give me wisdom and help me grow to be more Christ-like."

A sign of immaturity is a grudge. It is that chip on your shoulder that you don't want healed. You want to keep that spot pink. You want to because you want others to see it. You want to keep it so you can keep looking at it. You think it is a spot that will remind you not to trust, to keep up your walls. You think it is a protective mechanism. How silly that belief is. That grudge spot is not helping you. It makes you ugly. It calluses you. It is an abrupt rough spot in your life that people hate stumbling upon. It doesn't suit you.

To you who have grudges: let it go. Forgive, and you will be healed. Forgiveness will be like rotating that spot in which you have wanted to keep pink or rusted, and letting the light of Christ shine upon it. Seeking consistency in your life is to seek holiness. Refusing to do so is the second don't Paul warns us about:

2) Don't give the devil an opportunity.

We hold onto grudges when we are angry, when we are bothered. Anger is a natural human response. It is an emotion we can't help but get, but it is an emotion we can properly handle when we have gotten it. Those who hold on to anger when it arrives, decide to keep it locked inside. That is not where anger belongs. Anger is meant to be felt, then dealt with. People who hold grudges hold anger inside that they don't want dealt with. Never dealing with something is always the wrong solution because it is no solution.

Being angry is not a sin. Paul says it very clearly in verse 26 - "Be angry." BE it. He's saying feel it. Don't try to pretend you don't get angry. Don't pretend people don't upset you and bother you. It's okay! BUT, Paul goes on to say you must DEAL with your anger. The end of verse 27: "Do not let the sun go down while you are still angry." Let me make it ultra clear in case that didn't: Do not deny Jesus the right to address you when you have a problem. You know what he wants to do. He wants to forgive that person. He wants them to be free and you too. And this isn't what you want. We humans don't like to forgive. We think it makes us look weak. We think it lets down a wall to vulnerability. We want to cling to anger with all our might, rather than give someone grace. Saying "sorry" is likely to kill some of us. But to let Jesus speak to you about your problem will mean you will have to listen to him tell you to forgive, to love them just as he loves you.

Jesus wants you to speak the truth with your neighbor. He wants you to do this because he knows it will keep the bond of peace. It will cultivate unity. It will keep the body together, mended and unhindered by walls of bitterness. He knows that together we are harder to destroy. Where there is anger, there is dissension and where there is dissention Satan likes to weasel in.

A grudge is a wide open door for Satan. He will ride through your anger like a boat on a tidal wave. Anger, if left unresolved, becomes uncontrollable. It spouts off exactly what it feels in the moment. That wide open door is our mouth. It is where unwholesome words find their exit sign. It is where the name-calling flies. It is where things you wish you could take back, come darting out like rockets.

If you don't want to look back and say, "I wish I had never said that. I wish I hadn't done that. I wish I would have controlled my temper . . ." Then let the grudge go. Rotate toward the Son and mature up.

"But Kamra," you say, "they won't admit they hurt me. They'll never say sorry even if I do."

WHO CARES?!

Forgiveness is an act of healing. If they elect not to take it, that is on them. But you, you can heal. You can say your peace. You can explain it all. You can go back to that day and rehash it. You can cry and spill your guts and guess what, they might not even blink an eye. They might call you sensitive and that you need to toughen up. Been there. Done that. But don't let that stop you. They don't understand what true toughness looks like. You, in your vulnerability, just became the strongest person in the room. You are the courageous one. You are the bigger person if you can forgive and move on, if you can say sorry and reconcile. A tremendous amount of ripening will happen for you if you move forward with this. Trust me. You got this!

3) Don't grieve the Holy Spirit.

This is the last bit of advice Paul gives to wrap up this explanation on how to live in holiness. The Holy Spirit is that sweet voice inside you, spurring you on to forgive and love your neighbor, even when you don't want to. To grieve him is to ignore him. It is to shush him. It is to push down that gut feeling. It is to choke back the words, "I forgive you and I love you," when you see that grudge-giver.

Grieving the Holy Spirit is straight up refusing to grow in Christ. It is knowing you should do or say something in order to display God, but choosing yourself instead.

Grieving the Holy Spirit is like seeing the sunshine but saying you want to stay in the shade a little longer. It is choosing to live in darkness when you could be ripening in the sun. It is satisfying the cravings of your sinful flesh instead of the Spirit.

If you don't want to grieve the Holy Spirit, then you have to take a chance. You have to put yourself out there as the kind one, the compassionate one, the forgiving one.

I know it is scary and sounds counter-culture, but that is what Jesus does and that is who we should be like.

3. Live in Love

This section will be the shortest - NOT that is the easiest! But this imperative can be so simple. How do we live in love? We imitate God. We live as Jesus lived. That's all I need to say here. Perfect love is God for God is love. Jesus was God made flesh. Read about him. Follow his example. There. Done. Bam.

This is easy to say, but very hard to do. The love of God is not a wishy-washy-do-whatever-you-want-however-you-want kind of love. How did Jesus show God he loved him? How did he show us? Look at 5:2. He made himself a sacrificial and fragrant offering to God.

So first, we must love God and others as a sacrificial offering. This is one that takes sacrifice. Duh, Kamra. In the Old Testament it was giving the very best of what you had - the best in the herd, unblemished, healthy, beautiful, your favorite. It wasn't giving God your scraps. It wasn't giving him your leftovers. It was giving him your prized possession. To give any less wouldn't be a sacrifice at all.

Thus, for us to love God as a sacrificial offering, we offer him all we can of our very best. We offer him ourselves. We offer him the most treasured part of our being - our heart. What he wants from us is to "love the Lord our God with our heart, soul and strength" (Matthew 22:37). So we love him with everything we've got. Not just a Sunday kind of love. Not just when others are looking kind of love. It is all our muscles, all our mind, kind of teeth-gritting, keep on reaching, kind of love.

It means we give to others even when it hurts. We give to others our very best. When they ask for a cloak, we don't just give them the one in the back of the closet that has holes and missing buttons. We give them our nicest one. It means when they ask for forgiveness for hurting you, we give them another chance. We give them the grace that God freely gave us. We give them another shot at our heart. We love them with arms open wide, heart-exposed, ready to embrace them kind of love. We sacrifice our own desires when we want to stay clammed up, selfish, and number one. We forfeit the position of first and choose last. Sounds easy?

Secondly, we love God and others as a fragrant offering. This is the aroma a burnt offering would give off. Have you ever cooked steak on the grill? It smells so good! The smell of it could waft from your neighbor's cookout and make your mouth water a mile away. Now, on the other hand, have you ever cooked cabbage? Gag! It stinks up the whole house! You basically have to cook in a Hazmat suit. While I love my green veggies, the point should be clear: When you give your best it should have a pleasing aroma to everyone around you.

People can recognize when you haven't given your best. They can tell when you give them a candle that is fifteen years old. They can tell when you serve them sloppy seconds or have slaughtered the fattened calf. People can sniff out a fake compliment, a backhanded accolade, a joke that is made at their expense. Likewise, God can tell when we're just blowing smoke his way. He can tell when we're serving to be served, singing to be heard, praying to make a show, using him and offering him empty promises.

There's a short way to fix giving stinky offerings: be authentic, genuine and thankful. A thankful heart gives out of abundance. A genuine heart acts out of pure intentions. An authentic person speaks the truth in love.

There you have it. It was short and simply stated, but don't believe for one second that it is going to be an easy commission. Live in love. Let's try together.

4. Live in Light

There's two illustrations in scripture that you need to grasp before you understand this imperative to live in light. First, you need to know that Jesus is the Light. Second, you need to know that darkness is where Christ is not; it is sin.

Jesus announced to the human race "I am the light of the world! The one who follows me will never walk in darkness, but will have the light of life" (John 8:12). This is recorded by John who opened his gospel with this: "The true light, who gives light to everyone, was coming into the world" (John 1:9). Jesus was coming to make it perfectly clear where people should go - to the Father.

There are so many references coming to mind right now to make this illustration come to life. I can think of the Wisps Merida follows in the movie *Brave*. I can think of another Disney classic, *Sleeping Beauty*, where Aurora follows the glow of Maleficent to the spindle. But before I start naming a billion movies where people follow lights around, note the obvious: People follow light. Why? Because people are drawn to it. We don't naturally like the darkness because we can't see in the darkness. We, and maybe I should speak more of myself here, like to know what is ahead. We like to be aware of our surroundings.

I personally don't like driving through fog. It happens almost every morning for me because I live on a hilltop and I have to drive through a valley. It is in the valley that fog usually settles before rising. By the time it rises to the point of my hill it usually has dissipated. Fog is thickest in the valleys. It brings a whole new perspective to the fourth verse of Psalm 23. "Even though I must walk through the valley of the shadow of death..." I have to drive through this death trap nearly every day.

The headlights on my car are a life-saver. I put them on dim when I'm in the fog of that valley and I'm able to see about twenty feet at a time. Their light breaks through the fog just far enough for me to keep creeping forward. If I didn't have those headlights, I wouldn't be able to drive my daughter to school, at least not safely.

Jesus is our headlights. He is the one who shows us the way forward. He shows us where to turn, when to stop, if there's a bump, or in my case - a deer in the road. Without Jesus we'd be driving aimlessly in the fog, in the darkness, in valleys of death, hopeless and afraid.

People without lights to follow, or illuminate their paths, get lost. We become easy prey for the lions who prowl around at night looking for someone to devour. We are sitting ducks. It is in the darkness that evil elects to live.

Some people choose darkness. They want their deeds to be hidden from view. They want who they are or what they've done to stay secretive, especially from God. Like Adam and Eve when they first discovered they had sinned, people like to hide in the brush when they are ashamed. They flee from God's presence and cower alone. I don't know how many times I need to stop and say how dangerous this is. When people are alone they are in far greater danger to be killed by the Enemy.

When you're in darkness you don't care who's around you. You couldn't see them even if you knew they were there. Two people stumbling around in the pitch dark isn't any better than one person doing the same thing. It doesn't matter how many people are there with you, darkness is darkness and there's no seeing through it unless you have the Light of the world.

People who choose to stay in darkness are choosing to waste their lives. They are choosing to stay asleep when they could be awake and enjoying a beautiful day. You know what I'm talking about here. You know that person, or maybe you are that person, who could sleep past noon even though the sun is shining and the birds are singing. Growing up on a farm this was never allowed. To sleep through the day was a total waste of your time. The sunlight brought a glorious resource. We could see so we could chore! The sun was up so we were up. The animals need to be fed, the garden needs tending, the flowers need watering... All the things had to be done in the daylight. Trying to hoe a pumpkin patch at midnight would have resulted in butchered vines and dead plants. Certain work can only successfully be done in the daylight.

For this reason, Paul inserts an Old Testament imperative perfectly suited for this commission to live in light. He says, "Awake, O sleeper! Rise from the dead, and Christ will shine on you!" (Ephesians 5:14) Stop sleeping and wasting away this life. Stop plopping yourself down in the same pew Sunday after Sunday and never letting a single sermon infiltrate your life. Stop hiding in shame and trust again. Stop living in sin and pursue the way of Christ. Your life will be wasted if spent doing anything else.

Brothers and sisters, flee from darkness. That which you are keeping hidden, expose it to the light. He's here to help you get through the valley. It is never fun to have to go through them but at least when you're a Christian you have the Light of the World navigating your path. That is a luxury those who are lost don't have. For you and I, we believers, we can know the top of the hill is just around the corner and Jesus will guide us safely there. How sweet to trust in Jesus. How relieving, hands off the wheel freeing. We shouldn't want others to live without such comfort. If your headlights bring a wandering soul into view, pull over and strap them in. The greatest ride of their life is about to begin - a drive into sunny paradise.

5. Live Wisely

Jesus lived so wisely. He only had three years in ministry, showing everyone exactly who he was and what he was capable of doing. In that short time he did more things than his disciples could ever record. John ended his gospel like this, "There are many other things Jesus did. If every one of them were written down, I suppose the whole world would not have room for the books that would be written" (John 21:25). He truly took advantage of every opportunity.

If anyone was up and at em' in the mornings, it was Jesus. He used every ounce of daylight to glorify his father. He got to work and didn't stop. He had an urgency about him. He knew what was at stake - life or death. He didn't take it lightly. He poured into his friendships. He taught. He was in synagogues. He walked for miles. He met the needs of others. He went out of his way. He spent time at people's homes. He had dinner with sinners. He washed feet.

It doesn't all sound glamorous, what Jesus did. He chose to spend his time putting others first. He didn't use his three years of ministry to make a big name for himself. He didn't demand his disciples build him a temple or a castle or a mansion. He didn't have them start running his campaign and plastering his face on billboards. He did the opposite of all that. He didn't waste time having a home. They camped out. He didn't want any earthly possessions to slow him down. He didn't advertise his miracles. When he healed someone he told them to keep it on the down low. When a demon recognized him he commanded them to keep their slimy mouths shut. He didn't try to buy the favor of the Pharisees or get on the good side of Roman authorities. He kept his plow to the ground. So much to harvest and so few workers.

How do we spend our time?

I can't tell you how much time I got back when I deleted all my social media accounts. I used to mindlessly scroll through feeds and look at other people's pictures while sitting on my butt, ignoring my daughter, forgetting I had things to do, and watching the dishes stack. So silly. It was a total waste of time for me. I don't miss it even one little bit. Goodbye, Social Media. Hello, Bible.

That is just one example. Each year at Lent I give up something in order to spend that time reflecting on the Passion. A lot of people do it. It is meant to be a time to reprioritize. It is meant to be a season of sacrifice so we can experience a tiny fragment of the sacrifice our Lord went through on our behalf. If Lent is practiced, it is time well spent. It is a wise decision.

For me, it always feels like people pop into my life at inopportune times. A friend will want a phone chat right when I am finally getting a moment to myself. A neighbor will drop by right when I am about to finish a task and I have to stop. My grandma has the greatest knack at calling and wanting me to visit on the day I had planned to write or go shopping. In those moments I want so badly to say no, that I'm busy, to come back later. But I have found when I say yes and put that person before myself, it turns out to be the most rewarding. That is the day my friend would open up their heart about an issue. That is the day my neighbor would ask for prayer or about church service times. That is the day my grandma would do the funniest thing that I'd never forget, or fall and I'd be there to catch her. And to think if I had said no.

There's a small window for harvest. If you don't act right when the harvest is ready, you miss out. Take our family cherry trees for example. When they decide to come on you better be ready to pick. All those tiny sweet berries are ripe and ready to eat all within a week. If you don't get to them fast enough, the birds will, the squirrels will, the neighbors will, everyone will except you. Gone on vacation that one week in the summer? You missed them. Too busy to pick and pit? Your loss. The harvest is fleeting and you have to be willing and ready to work.

A wise person knows the skill of prioritizing. A wise person knows the damage of procrastination. A farmer knows when to harvest. A Christian ought to know when to submit to others out of reverence for Christ.

Be wise with your time. People that are here today could be gone tomorrow. Your opportunity to share the gospel has a window. When you see a person is receptive, like freshly tilled soil, you need to plant the Good News!

Practice the words of Jesus recorded in Matthew 10:16:

> *Be as shrewd as snakes*
> *and innocent as the doves.*

When the Serpent saw his opportunity to influence Eve and Adam in the Garden, he took it! In the same way, he needed to be on the lookout and strike when the opportunity presents itself. Being as shrewd as a snake will mean we are in position for an opportunity to talk about and show Jesus. In conjunction with that, we need to be as tender as doves when that opportunity comes along. Satan, disguised as the serpent, definitely wasn't that. But he had good tactics. We need to combine that wisdom with the gentleness of the Holy Spirit.

When you see the chance, take it! When the chance is in your hand, be soft with it. Don't be like Tommy Boy. Chris Farley held his dinner roll in his hand and explained to his friend, Richard - David Spade, and the waitress, why he was doing so poorly at selling brake pads. When he had a sale in his hand he got too excited - "Like Joe-Joe the Indian circus boy with a pretty new pet!" He destroyed it by being too abrasive. That's when he blows it. If he had just stayed calm, holding, petting and stroking his pretty new pet, it would have worked out. That dinner roll would have been lovingly savored rather than end up in crumbs across the table. If you have no idea what I'm talking about right now, just watch that scene from *Tommy Boy*. It's the best.

My point is: Combine the wisdom of the snake with the tenderness of the dove. Seize every opportunity and harvest it with the utmost care. Pounce on the cherry tree when it is ready, but place each soft cherry gently into the bucket. In the same way, recognize the dinner roll placed in your hands as the soft, easily destroyable, piece of bread that it is. Don't let it go to waste and don't tear it up. God's putting people into your path at just the right time. Make eye contact with them and smile like you mean it. Forge ahead. You're going to nail that sale next time!

6. Live Spiritually Aware & Armored

Jesus was able to live so wisely, making the most of every opportunity, exuding in holiness, love and light, and bringing people together in unity because he recognized the spiritual world in this physical place. Where some saw a terrible tax collector, Jesus saw Matthew - a fellow disciple and friend. Where society saw crazy men who needed to be chained in the outskirts, Jesus saw demons ready to flee. Where Pharisees saw a paralytic, Jesus saw the heart of a man who needed forgiveness of sins. His eyes went beyond this physical realm. Jesus was always keenly aware of the spiritual.

Until we recognize there is a spiritual dimension, a battle ongoing between evil and good, we stand bare-assed, empty-handed, and sure to die by our Enemy. Apples who hang and claim, "I don't believe worms exist," are sure to get their bottoms eaten out from under them and their guts will fall through their butts. That's a pretty picture, huh?

Wake up, Christians! There's a real war going on all around you. You might not believe you're worth a fight from the enemy, but trust me, he wants to bite into you as much as the next apple. "I'm just a nobody from Canaan," you may say to yourself, "No devil is going to pick a fight with me. He's got bigger fish to fry." LIES! Satan isn't just going for the pastors, the nonprofit starters, the missionaries, the big shot Politician or social media influencer. He's going for all of us because, no matter how small the town, how young or how old you are, how rich or how poor, we all have equal opportunity at impacting the kingdom of Christ just as much as the next guy does.

I used to believe that lie. I believed the enemy wouldn't waste his time on me. I believed I was too small, too womanly, too simple to ever be bothered with. Then it all became abundantly clear one day: I was under a spiritual attack that had finally bubbled over to physical consequences. I couldn't ignore it any longer. I had to admit it: Satan was trying to kill me.

I may never be a pastor. I may never be someone you see on a television screen sharing the gospel with millions of viewers. I probably won't ever go viral. People outside of my hometown will probably never even know my name. This book might sell a whopping ten copies. But I still have the light of Christ. I still know God's Word and I have a mouth that can speak and hands that can type. I have the ability to share with my neighbors, my friends, my family, and with strangers that Jesus loves them. And guess what, Satan hates that. He wants me dead, and if you have the same heart and ability to share the Gospel, he wants to murder you as well.

When we live with the constant awareness that there is something bigger than this physical world, we live differently. When we remember people could go to hell or be tormented by demons if we don't share God's love with them, we don't care to go shopping for the hundredth time. We don't care if the jeans are designer or not. We don't care if the steak is medium or well done. Who cares in light of it all? Does it really matter if that girl has better sneakers than you when she might be overwhelmed by a spirit of inadequacy? Does your job performance or attendance record matter when someone you care about may die and not have accepted Jesus as their Lord?

People, people, people. Apples, apples, apples. I'm telling you. When you live with spiritual eyes, the physical stuff doesn't matter so much. And when we have spiritual eyes, a lot of the physical problems we thought we had are suddenly discovered for what they actually are - demons masquerading around. When we are able to properly identify a spiritual battle, we are properly equipped to fight it.

So first, stop and ask God to give you spiritual awareness. Ask him to open your eyes so you may identify where an enemy is lurking. After you have prayed this, go forward with your everyday tasks with the knowledge that your real fight is a spiritual one, not a physical one. Your fight is not against your neighbor. It is not against your boss, or Ms. Popular, or your evil step-mother. Your battle is not against the chewing tobacco, the alcohol bottle, the lustful urges, or the computer screen. It is deeper than that. They are pawns. The real enemy is behind them, using them. He's been hiding there. Lock eyes with him now and call him out.

"Our struggle is not against flesh and blood, but against the rulers, against the powers, against the rulers of this darkness, against the spiritual forces of evil in the heavens."

No more trying to fight spiritual battles with physical weapons. You have been trying to crush that addiction of tobacco for years, to no avail. You've been trying to ignore those sexual urges, to countless failures. You've tried the medications, the talking, the tactics, the working out, the running, the accountability partners, the diets, the doctors... There's nothing wrong with that. God can use those things to help you. Praise God for them. But you need to go deeper than that. You can't do this on your own. You need to turn to the Holy Spirit. It is time to take a spiritual approach. Let's go.

1) Put on the belt of truth.

Fasten tightly around your waist who God says you are, who he says he is, and what is really going on in this physical world. Know the Word of God so when a lie is thrown your way you can watch it go by and land in the dirt. Let truth hold up your wardrobe. Let it be what keeps your outfit together. When people talk to you they ought to know you won't give one syllable of a lie. You are not the rumor-starter. You squish bugs of deception. When people tug at you trying to rip off your shirt of holiness, hurt your image, or make you go back on your word, tighten your belt even tighter.

2) Put on the breastplate of righteousness.

A breastplate guards the heart. Our hearts are so sensitive. We can be heartbroken so easily. Some of us even tend to wear our hearts on our sleeves. We let them be completely exposed. I understand this. I've ripped my heart out and offered it to people without much hesitation. I've gotten hurt multiple times for this too.

Our hearts are precious. We should be more careful with them. We shouldn't give them away to just anyone. We need to take protective measures. If the wrong people get a hold of our hearts, there's going to be severe damage. If the enemy takes hold of it, he's bound to stab it.

Putting on a breastplate of righteousness is putting on a filter that all things must process through before it penetrates our heart.

Think of the breastplate of righteousness like your heart's bodyguard. He stands there and asks everything a series of questions before he allows it in your heart. "Are you true? Are you worthy of respect? Are you just, pure, lovely, commendable, excellent and praiseworthy?" (Philippians 4:8) If they can't answer those questions positively, then they aren't on the list. Access denied.

If you're letting just any old junk into your life, you are not utilizing the bodyguard. You give him the day off when you decide to hook up with Joe Shmoe. You say he needs a day at the cleaners when you elect to binge on garbage television. You think a few things won't cause that much damage to your heart, but you're sadly mistaken. You let in one little worm and he will wreak havoc. You get him out and he's bound to bring seven more friends with him next time. He knows you're an easy target and he even knows what days you choose to give your bodyguard the day off. Don't.

3) Put on shoes of peace.

Paul words this like so: "Fit your feet with the preparation that comes from the good news of peace." He's saying you need to be ready to fight spiritual battles by having a readiness about you. You need to be prepared to act, to go, to fend yourself, to protect your fellow brothers and sisters who are in this battle alongside you. How do you do that?

Have you ever prepared for battle? If you're a military personnel, I applaud you. I can't imagine getting ready to face a man with a machine gun, or stare down an incoming tank. When a commander gives the sign for you to get into position, I can only imagine being overrun with anxiety, adrenalin. Thank you for your service.

If you haven't fought in military combat, maybe you can remember that feeling you got when you had to give the big presentation. When you had to start the game with the ball and there were only seconds left on the clock. When you took your vows. When you waited with your breath held for their answer. We've all had those moments when you had to brace yourself. We've all seen the upcoming task and wondered how we were going to handle it, how it was going to go, how it would be received, what they would think.

I've recently been watching the movie *Braveheart*. As the opposing army lined up at the other end of the field, I remember thinking, "How does William Wallace look so calm?" The way he stood there so stoic, calm, not shivering or backing away an inch, made me believe his character was ready to die for what he believed in. He had no doubts he wanted to be there. He had every belief that what he was fighting for was the right thing. So he stood firm.

This is what Paul is commissioning us to do: "Stand against the schemes of the devil. Take up the full armor of God so that you may be able to stand your ground. Stand firm therefore!" Three times he says it, three verses in a row.

We stand on our feet. (I know - sometimes I say the most obvious things.) Our feet take us places. Our feet get us from point A to point B. Our feet are so important. They must be well-taken care of. When researching the gear I would need for a hobby called "through hiking," I learned one of the most, if not the most important, pieces is your footwear. If you don't have comfortable shoes, or shoes fitted for the environment you're going to walk in, you won't make it very far.

Brothers and sisters, we won't make it far in this world if we aren't fitted with shoes of peace. We won't be able to stand as William Wallace did if we aren't overwhelmed with a sense of peace, that where we are is exactly where we are meant to be and what we're standing for is 100% right. If you're doubting the message of Christ is true and freeing, you won't present the Gospel with assurance. You'll stutter and freak out and sweat and try to change the subject. You have to be sure that what you're standing in is the most peaceful, life-giving message you could ever have the privilege of sharing.

Walk about with shoes of peace. Whistle a tune, "Blessed assurance. Jesus is mine. He can be yours too." Slip on your peace-sandals. Tighten the laces of your calm-cleats. You'll be able to enjoy a long, uphill climb in those brands.

4) Put on the Shield of faith.

Have you ever encountered an obstacle and thought there is no way I'm getting through that? When Frodo, Gollum and Sam arrived at the black gate of Mordor, Sam looked at the giant wall and said, "We can't get past that." It was a mighty fortress. It was built to keep people out and certain people in. The bigger the wall, the bigger the statement. This particular wall in *The Lord of the Rings - The Two Towers*, said, "Impossible. You can't get over me. You can't break through me. There's no way around me, or under me. This is where you stop." That is one heck of a wall.

We need to be seen by our enemies as a mighty wall like that. We need to have faith so strong it looks like a shield that no enemy could ever get through. Our faith needs to be so well built that the enemy just looks at us and thinks, "Do I even try?"

We need to show these demons we are locked up tight. We ask them, "You want in? Too bad, so sad," we say. "You're going to try to shove me over?" We raise an eyebrow at their pathetic approach. "HA! Your arrows will bounce off me like twigs. I'm solid. My foundation was laid at birth. I've been building on this wall of faith for years. You can't tear me down with a single blow. You're going to have to bring a whole army. You're going to have to bring bigger cannons. I'm not coming down easy, and definitely not without a fight."

See how important having a strong faith is? It is our line of defense. Without this shield we are exposed and helpless. We can fling around a sword of the Word but one single unblocked arrow from the Devil will take us out if we don't have a shield of faith. Never stop working on building this. Make it stronger. Pour more concrete into it. Add more rocks. Spend more time reading scripture. Attend more bible studies. Participate in church. Go on mission trips. Grow. Grow. Grow and don't stop. Your faith can never be too big, your shield too protective.

5) Put on the helmet of salvation.

Just like our hearts, our minds are a vital organ that need extra protection. Shoot me in the leg and I'm likely to live. Cut off my arm and I bet I can make it. But stab me in the heart or bash out my brains and I give it a 0% chance of survival. So like our breastplate, we must put on a helmet to protect what goes into our minds.

If the enemy has control of your thoughts, he will have control of your actions. If the enemy can get in your head and take charge of what you think about - how you view yourself, how you imagine the world sees you, what you believe about God - then you are screwed. You've just given him control of what you say and why you say it. You are no longer yourself. You're a slave.

When Satan makes you a slave you become obedient to sin. You live to die. When you give your mind to God, he makes you a son or daughter, an heir to the throne, a victor, a champion. Galatians 4:7 says, "You are no longer a slave, but a son, and if you are a son, then you are also an heir through God." When you place your mind in a helmet of salvation you are placing your mind in Christ's hands. You are no longer a slave to sin, but a slave unto Jesus. I know that it can be scary to hear we are slaves to someone, but don't you see that to be a slave for Jesus is still the best thing we could be? When we are slaves to Christ we aren't beaten by him to do his work. We aren't whipped into shape if we are lousy Christians. He is the perfect Master and when we know him in his perfection it is the easiest and most pleasurable thing to be his servant.

When your mind is a slave to the enemy the payoff is death. When you give your mind to the saving work of Jesus, your gift is eternal life (Romans 6:22-23).

Knowing that you are God's and you're saved gives you the insight to come into battle as having already overcome it. When your mind is at rest in the helmet of knowing you are saved, you don't worry about tomorrow. You don't worry about the devil's schemes. You are sealed for the day of redemption. Everything becomes a win-win scenario.

My grandmother has been in and out of the hospital for months this year. Every time she gets better she seems to get another sickness and she's down again. Through these hospital stays I've had the privilege of seeing her in joy despite it all. In her hospital bed she told me she'd be happy to go to her physical home and rest in her easy chair again, but she'd also be more than happy to go to her heavenly home too. Living or dying - for her, it is a win-win. That's the beautiful perspective we get to live in each time we slip on the helmet of salvation. It'll make all your battles look differently.

6) Put on the cloak of zeal.

I know this one isn't listed in the Ephesians passage, but it is still in the Bible. It is one of my favorites too so it is going to get mentioned whether you like it or not.

Zeal: to be filled with enthusiasm, gumption, excitement, passion. Zeal is like a lightning bolt. It is that extra kick. It is an energy drink that tops off your lunch. It is the punch, the bam, the ka-pow! Zeal is the decorative cape no superhero actually needs, but boy does it look great!

Perhaps that is why Paul doesn't mention it in his letter. You don't actually need zeal. It doesn't protect you and it doesn't help you fight better. But zeal can still add something really powerful. It adds character. It makes a statement. Cloaks draw attention. It might just add more soldiers to your army.

All throughout history you'll find people who wore cloaks to show their authority, their power, their position, their elegance. Cloaks were a fancy thing back in the day. People could barely afford underwear, much less a giant piece of extra material that draped down their back. People who wore cloaks drew the eye.

When you wear zeal for the Lord you captivate people's attention. Not for yourself, but for God's glory. When you show excitement for the Gospel, people wonder why. They start to get excited themselves. Joy rubs off on people. If you're laughing and smiling and sharing the message of Jesus with glee, others will want it!

I know all of us will go about this differently. Some of us are more shy than others. Some of us absolutely hate attention. We don't want anyone to look at us. Wearing a cloak of zeal may sound too flashy. But there are ways to wear your cloak of zeal comfortably. You don't have to scream and dance during worship service. You don't have to beat the pulpit while you preach. There are other ways. You could light up every time you get to pray for someone. You could bring your finest bunch of flowers to your sick neighbor with a ribbon tied on the vase and a get well card with your best calligraphy. You could serve that customer their cup of coffee but add, "I hope you have a blessed day," with your most sincere smile. That is a touch of zeal, my friend. Wear it proudly. I guarantee others will join the fight.

7) Put on the sword of the Spirit.

This lovely weaponry was already discussed in a previous chapter. I hope it was helpful to you. Here, I just want to recap that this sword is a device meant to help you fight off the enemy, not cut down fellow Christians or innocent civilians. The Word of God is sharp and distinctive. It has power to slay a demon, but it also has power to sever a sister in Christ.

Unfortunately, Christians have been known to wave around the Word of God in careless fashion. They throw out verses as if they're arrows to pin someone's demon to the ground, when they could actually just puncture someone. A skilled warrior for Christ needs to have the ability to discern where an evil spirit needs to be sleighed with the truth and where a lost soul needs a sheathed, listening friend.

Keep your sword ready. Have your hand gripped on that Bible, ready to pull at any moment. Have verses in your mind. But don't fling that sword around at every living thing that comes your way. People don't need to be cut down, the Devil does.

We've reached the end. The pieces of the armor are laid out for you. Now I ask you: Do you want to be ready to handle what life throws at you? Want to be ready to fight those pesky worms? To be dropped and not bust on the earth? To be pressured by others and not bruised? There's a miracle skin cream here to make you baby soft but impenetrably thick-skinned. It is composed from these six ingredients - unity, holiness, love, light, wisdom and this final one, spiritual awareness and the armor. Apply this daily in a generous heaping and you're bound to have skin like Jesus.

Chapter 6 Reflection

1. In Ephesians Paul gives six pieces of advice to those who want to live as Christ (unity, holiness, love, light, wisdom, spiritually aware and armored). Which of them do you feel you need to work on most and why?

2. Within the section on holiness three don't's are given. If you reversed the wording to do's how would you put it? Explain.

3. Seven pieces of armor are listed under the "Live Spiritually Aware & Armored" section. Which of them do you find most helpful to you in your current season and why?
Tough skin isn't what the world thinks it is.
Label the illustration with the pieces of armor and advice of Paul.

Chapter 6 Challenge

Choose one (Or all three if you want to bulk up!) to complete:

1) Dig into Ephesians chapter 6. Print it out and mark it up. I suggest you:
- Highlight your favorite parts.
- Circle the pieces of armor.
- Ask a question of each piece of armor and search for the answers in commentaries, resources, and through wise counsel.
- Underline your tasks.
- Make notes. Keep this in your bible or journal.

2) Study the book of Ephesians. You could:
- Find a study material that goes with the book.
- Do a group study or partner with someone to go through it with you.
- Write out the book word for word in a journal.
- Print it out and mark it up.

3) If you avoided the challenge of giving up a grudge in the previous chapter, you are about to encounter it again. Grudges are wounds that make our skin ugly, rough to the touch. It is time to let it heal and become smooth.
Go to the person you have built up a wall against and grant them forgiveness. You are not granting them permission or access to hurt you, but you are freeing yourself up from the anger and hostility you have kept inside.
If you cannot physically go to them, write them a letter or send them an email.

If you can no longer connect with them, write it all out in formatting of your choosing and imagine giving it to them. Say everything you fear you couldn't say in person. Then be free from the anger that is tied with them. It is time to let it go.

If you are doing this study with a small group, make time to discuss this challenge with them and encourage one another.

Chapter 7
Core & Stem

Do you ever eat the core of your apple? Of course not. You always eat round and round to that little hunk of middle and then you toss it away. No one wants to bite into the crunchy center and try to swallow down seeds as if they were fruit pills. Gross! But did you know, the core is the most nutritious part of the apple?

Today released an article in 2019 titled, "Study claims we've been eating apples wrong - here's why..."[4] It goes on to explain an apple has about 100 million bacterial cells that are good for humans to consume, but when we toss out the core we are actually only eating about 10 million of them. 90% of the nutrition we could gain from eating the fruit is in the core! Man, have we been missing out!

I'll never forget the day I learned I had been eating bananas wrong my whole life. Apparently, monkeys peel them from the opposite end of where humans traditionally do - from the stem. I couldn't believe I had been doing it wrong all those years. It really is easier to peel it from the other end. Sometimes that blasted stem doesn't want to snap away.

Let this be another day to go down in history as that crucial moment we learned we have been eating another fruit wrong all along.

The core is the most important part of the apple. It is what holds the apple together, gives it the shape and houses the seeds. Without a sturdy core, the apple would be formless, like a human without a spine. That's it! The core is like a spine. It is foundational. Without it,

---

[4] *Today.* Grant, Michelle. "Study Claims We've Been Eating Apples Wrong - Here's Why: Apparently the Peel isn't the most nutritious part of the apple." July 29, 2019. https://www.today.com/food/new-study-claims-we-ve-all-been-eating-apples-wrong-t159751

the fruit could not be a fruit. Without it, the fruit would not exist.

What is our core? What holds us up and keeps us together? What is foundational to who we are? What is that part of our being that without it, we would mush and be formless?

I have an answer.

Our core is our morality. It is what makes us human. It is what gives us shape and definition. Like a spine, it is the principles that keep us straight. Without some form of morality, we are wishy-washy, mushy, and our existence is meaningless.

People without a strong core tend to bend and adjust their shape for anyone who comes along. One day they can be a tall, round apple and the next they can be a pancake of a shape just laying around and letting everything pass over them. In front of their Pastor they are sturdy and mature. In front of their coworkers they are concave and infantile. In front of their boss, or their best friend, or their new beau, they are spineless. They do whatever with whoever for whatever cost because they have no morality to tell them otherwise. They are coreless. They are the apples who make other apples go, "Hypocrisy! Liar! Fake! Phony! All for show! Back-stabber! Inauthentic!"

Then, before you know it, apples choose to not to have the same fake core those hypocritical apples said they had. Why would they choose it when it appears to be a core that caves at the slightest pressure?

Shifting our core for those we are in front of is like changing our outfit to suit that person's taste. For example: My boss is coming - change my core of morality, put on the professional blazer and tie. Forget loving my enemies, let's crush the competition with some shady business deals. Or: That gorgeous man is coming my way - change my core of morality and slip into the slimming, sleazy, strapless dress. Forget waiting until marriage and not tripping up my brothers in Christ, I'm going to do whatever is needed to hear him say I'm the most beautiful and desirable.

People do it all the time. They profess a core of Christianity but when push comes to shove, or an idol demands our allegiance, we melt. We toss out the core and change our garments to fit the situation. Unfortunately, it is this inability to stand firm with our core that has projected to unbelievers that the Christian morale is weak and an inferior choice from all the options of cores in this world.

People don't want cores that crumble. People don't want to have to change every time someone new comes around. They want to be themselves, at all times. Changing is exhausting. If a new outfit was required for every person, we'd all choose to be nudist. We want to be proud of who we are. To step out in our sweatpants and say, "This is me. Take it or leave it." People want cores that don't change. And you'll actually find that people respect others who refuse to change their cores, even if their outfits don't match everyone else.

So what are we projecting to the world? Are we Christians an unashamed, unabashed generation that will proudly wear our cross tattoos and helmets of salvation? Are we a people with an unshakeable, unmoving core? For those of us who cannot answer "yes," we are in grave danger.

Any apple without a firm core will decay. Any Christian without their foundation firmly laid in Christ, will also decay. Jesus gave this very warning. It is recorded in Matthew 7. He used the illustration of a foolish man building his house on the sand versus a wise man building his rock on the rock. The foolish man was unwise because he did not listen to the words of God, the words of Jesus. Instead, he ignored the words and went on doing whatever he wanted, wherever he wanted, with whatever and whoever. He was careless. He was paying attention to his own desires instead of listening to the Spirit. So when heavy rains came and winds beat against his house, it caved in. Just like that - destroyed.

Likewise, humans who don't heed the Word of God are stupid. Was that harsh of me? What else does it mean to be "unwise?" Idiotic, dim-witted, thick, brainless . . . That's what Jesus was saying. We are stupid if we hear God's word and choose to do our thing instead. Plain stupid. Do you want to be stupid? I sure don't!

A stupid person looks at sand and thinks, "That's a great place to build a house!" I'm no architect, or builder, or carpenter, but this I know: sand moves. It goes in and out with the waters that come in with the tides. It is there one second and gone the next. It is recycled from the ocean. It is lightweight and can be carried off with a gentle breeze, much less a mighty wind. Those who choose to build on the oceanfront don't simply lay a foundation on the sand. They have to mix sand with water and ROCKS. They create concrete. A wise builder knows, rocks make all the difference.

Rocks

Rocks are hard. They are heavy. Quite often they are immovable. In large masses they are mountains. Mountains! Have you ever tried to move a mountain? Have you jumped on a rock? It doesn't move. It won't cave in. It won't crack. See a boulder in a stream and the water moves around it. It does not get moved by even the fastest currents. See the remarkable difference between sand and rock?

That is why God is referred to as the Rock in Scripture. He is ascribed the name because he is viewed as a fortress, a saving place that no enemy can break through. Over and over again the psalmist David ascribed this term to God. Don't believe me? It is in Psalm 18, 27, 28, 31, 40, 42, 61, 62, 71, 78, 81, 89, 92, 94, 95, 105, 114 and 118. That's just the Psalms.

Isaiah makes a bold prophetic word in regard to a rock. He prophesied a rock would be laid by God that would be "a tried stone, a precious cornerstone, a firm foundation" for whoever believes in it (28:16). This prophecy came true through the person of Jesus Christ. His apostle Peter quotes this in his letter to believers.

For it says in Scripture, "Look I lay in Zion a stone,
a chosen and precious cornerstone,
and whoever believes in him will never be put to shame."
1 Peter 2:6

He goes on to quote another Old Testament scripture - Psalm 118:

"The stone the builders rejected has become the
cornerstone." (verse 22)

He references these two verses to illustrate how Jesus fulfilled Isaiah's prophecy but even in his fulfillment, he was still rejected by some. Ironically, this is said from the very man who once rejected Christ three times and still, this man was simultaneously the one Jesus called "the rock." Yep, Peter was the first and original Dwayne Johnson!

Peter knew what it meant to reject Christ. He had done it before. On the night of Jesus' arrest, Peter denied having any connection with him three times. Afraid of being found out, being arrested, maybe even being crucified alongside Christ, Peter stepped off the foundation he had once stood so firmly on.

Rewind from this night of betrayal to earlier in Jesus' ministry. He stopped to ask his disciples who people said he was. Each took a turn giving their answers. "Some say John the Baptist, others Elijah, and others Jeremiah or one of the prophets." Jesus shook his head. "Who do you all think I am?" Peter, who then was called Simon, spoke up,

"You are the Christ, the Son of the living God." Jesus then blessed Simon son of Jonah and changed his name to Peter - Πέτρος- which means rock in Greek. Jesus said, on that rock, his church would be built and the gates of Hades would not overpower it. (Matthew 16:13-20)

Jesus recognized the statement of faith Peter had just made about him was not from himself, but revealed to Peter through the Spirit, through his Father in heaven. The fact that Jesus was the Messiah, the fulfillment of all prophecies, a part of the Trinity, was fundamental. The future of the church had to have the same statement of faith as that of Peter in order to be built up. Jesus was the Rock and the fact that Peter had recognized it meant the Spirit was in him, thus, the Rock was in him. A name change was necessary at that point. A new identity was taking hold of Simon. He was no longer a son of Jonah, but a son of God, a walker on the Rock.

When Peter stepped off this rock, he stumbled into lying and denying his own identity, along with his Identity-Giver - Jesus. Without that foundation, he crumbled. He fell into a mass of hysteria and started chopping off ears and yelling at people at campfires. He fell apart. He went back to fishing, lying around half naked in a boat. What he had once stood so firmly on was gone. He was spineless.

Then the day came. Jesus was spotted on the shore yelling at his friends to come in for breakfast. Peter saw him. He saw the Rock he had once walked with and upon. He wanted it back. He jumped out of the boat and swam across the lake to get to Jesus, the man he had betrayed. Jesus was alive, having risen from the dead. He was back to reinstate Peter. He took the stupid man, the one who went back to the sand instead of staying on the Rock, and he re-established him. "Do you love me? Do you love me? Do you really love me?" And with three "yeses," Peter was back on the Rock.

It was under this reinstatement Peter was able to tell the church they are now living stones. They are rocks too when they accept the Rock. Not just him. They too are chosen. They get to be a part of the body of Christ that is made of many living rocks, laid upon Him - the Founding Rock, the Precious Cornerstone. He says he used to be a normal person but then he was selected and set upon the Rock.

"You too were once not a people, but now you are God's people. You have been shown mercy."
1 Peter 2:10

Peter says you have been given an identity change.
"You are a chosen race, a royal priesthood, a holy nation, a people of his own."
1 Peter 2:9

Friends, if you have a core that is anything but Jesus being Lord, you will decay. If you're trying to build a life on the truth that you are your own god, your spouse is your god, your sexuality is your god, your money is your god, your job, your kids, your spirituality, your house, your car, your status, your title, your good works . . . you will crumble. Those things are fleeting. They are not everlasting. Heavy winds can blow them away. Deep waters can wash them away. But Jesus, he cannot be moved.

Cores made of gold, silver, precious stones, wood, hay or straw, will be plainly seen one day. When the storms of life come, they will be seen falling. When waters of trouble come, they will cry out for help or drown. That is what 1 Corinthians 3 talks about (verses 10-17). Paul goes on to say that the world thinks it is wise to build with flashy gold materials or striking silver, but what the world thinks is wise is actually stupid. A wise person knows a rock when they see one. A wise person heeds the Word of God.

So again, I ask: What is at your core? What is most important to you? What, when everything else is going horribly wrong, do you retreat to?

We all have to stand on something. We all need to be ready to give an answer when Jesus turns and asks, "Who do YOU say I am?" When coworkers, friends, family and even strangers start to poke at the core of you, what will you reveal? Are you ready to give an answer? Peter was, and Peter petitions us to have an answer ready at all times. He said,

"Set Christ apart as Lord in your heart
and always be ready to give an answer
to anyone who asks about the hope you possess."
1 Peter 3:15

How do you stay ready? Set Christ apart as Lord in your heart. That is what you stand on. That is your foundation. Jesus is Lord. He is the answer to all the questions. He is the reason why. He is the because. If he is Lord of our heart, we are living stones. We are walking talking rocks building up the body of Christ which is the Church, which Jesus is the foundation of.

Together, we should make up one mighty mountain of a mass! We should be an immovable force, one to be reckoned with. Enemies fire away. We will not crumble. What an amazing thing to be a part of! To not be alone. To not fight by ourselves. We are an army of living stones. We have each other. At least, that is how it is supposed to work . . .

Church, may I have a moment here? Are we taking this chapter to heart? Are we all making Christ the cornerstone? Are we all laid upon one Precious Foundation? If we are, then why are we pitted against one another? Why is there a church on the corner that hates the church on the river? Why is there a denomination claiming the other is heretical? Furthermore, why are there so many who say the church hurt them and turned them away from Jesus? Are we rocks that are stoning people, or providing them a firm landing when they fall to their Savior? We are living stones meant to build a great fortress to house the weak and wounded, to repair them and hope they become an additional rock to the castle of God's Sanctuary. We are not meant to build up in order to keep people out. We are a temple, not a wall. Thanks for giving me a moment. That's all.

If you are uncertain about your beliefs about Jesus, you need to work on that. If you want to be wise and build your house on the Rock, you must heed the Word of God. That means you need to read it. Yep, you need to read your Bible. You need to study it from top to bottom, front to back. You need additional resources. You need study materials, commentaries, people strong in their faith and knowledgeable. You need to ask Granny about that verse you don't understand. You need to take the Pastor aside if you didn't catch what he was explaining at the pulpit. You need to speak up in small group. You need to pray. You need to stop and listen for God's voice. You need to ask the Holy Spirit to help you understand. You need, you need, you need.

Why, Kamra? Why do so much work and need so much? Because your core is the most important part of you. What you believe is the most important part of you. A.W. Tozer put it this way, "What comes into our minds when we think about God is the most important thing about us." It is what gives us shape. It is what our identity hinges on. It is what takes us from a Simon to a Peter. So, if you want to know who you really are and what you are meant for, you must know what you think about God. To remain oblivious to this question, to stay in an agnostic limbo, is to remain empty and formless. Guess what, you were meant for much more than that.

I dare you to get to the core of yourself. I bet you find more purpose and meaning. I bet you will be changed for the better. You will be stronger and more secure when you put in that work I mentioned above. You will be one tasty looking apple! My hope for you is that you can have a clear definition of what is at your core. If someone asks you what you believe, I hope you can give it to them straight and clear every single time, just like Peter did. Have a faith statement ready. Be able to say, "My core is . . ." or "I am . . ."

A good example for such a faith statement could be the Nicene Creed. Check it out:

We believe in one God,
the Father almighty,
maker of heaven and earth,
of all things visible and invisible.
And in one Lord Jesus Christ,
the only Son of God,
begotten from the Father before all ages,
God from God,

Light from Light,
true God from true God,
begotten, not made;
of the same essence as the Father.
Through him all things were made.
For us and for our salvation
he came down from heaven;
he became incarnate by the Holy Spirit and the
virgin Mary,
and was made human.
He was crucified for us under Pontius Pilate;
He suffered and was buried.
The third day he rose again, according to the
Scriptures.
He ascended to heaven
and is seated at the right hand of the Father.
He will come again with glory
to judge the living and the dead.
His kingdom will never end.
And we believe in the Holy Spirit,
the Lord, the giver of life.
He proceeds from the Father and the Son,
and with the Father and the Son is worshiped and
glorified.
He spoke through the prophets.
We believe in one holy catholic and apostolic church.
We affirm one baptism for the forgiveness of sins.
We look forward to the resurrection of the dead,
and to life in the world to come. Amen.[5]

It covers the basics: God, Jesus and the Holy Spirit. That is a really good foundation. Maybe for you it

---

[5] *Nicene Creed.* (2021). Loyola Press.
https://www.loyolapress.com/catholic-resources/prayer/
traditional-catholic-prayers/prayers-every-catholic-should-know
/nicene-creed/ (Original work published 325)

is memorizing a piece of Scripture. The hymn to Christ is a good one:

In your relationships with one another, have the same
mindset as Christ Jesus:
Who, being in very nature God,
did not consider equality with God something to be
used to his own advantage;
rather, he made himself nothing
by taking the very nature of a servant,
being made in human likeness.
And being found in appearance as a man,
he humbled himself
by becoming obedient to death—
even death on a cross!
Therefore God exalted him to the highest place
and gave him the name that is above every name,
that at the name of Jesus every knee should bow,
in heaven and on earth and under the earth,
and every tongue acknowledge that Jesus Christ is Lord,
to the glory of God the Father.
Philippians 2:5-11

Or maybe you could memorize the lyrics of a song. Like "We Believe" by Newsboys:

We believe in God the Father
We believe in Jesus Christ
We believe in the Holy Spirit
And He's given us new life
We believe in the crucifixion
We believe that He conquered death
We believe in the resurrection
And He's coming back again
We believe

Bulk up on your core. Have a core day like you would in the gym. Every Monday, for example, decide you're going to strengthen your core. Take ten minutes to meditate. Take twenty minutes to read and memorize. Take thirty minutes to pray. You get the idea. When you invest that much work into it, you'll recognize how truly important it actually is to who you are. When you realize its importance I guarantee you'll want others to know it. When someone wants to know you on the deepest level of who you are, you'll want to share this core with them. That brings me to my next point: When you care about someone, you should want to know their core too.

Since the core holds the most nutritional value, when you get to the core of someone you are discovering the most intimate and important parts of that person - Why they are the way they are, why they believe what they believe, think what they think and feel what they feel. It goes beyond the surface level conversation of finding out they like videogames and peanut butter. It is discovering they have identity issues because of how they were raised or neglected by their father. It is learning they believe in God because of a moving experience at a summer camp many years ago that forever changed their heart.

People have a tendency to want to stay surface level. We don't mind showing people our skin, our Nike tennis shoes and concert t-shirts. But to get to the deep stuff, to go way in where it is personal and foundational, that is scary. We tend to keep people out of there. We get scared when they start to dig in. We choose to avoid the heavy topics, the political debates, the building blocks of our faith and upbringing, the daddy issues, the revolutionary retreat from our teen years that redirected our life. To bring all this up would mean a lengthy discussion where the opposite party is going to learn a whole lot about that person. We tend to avoid those kinds of talks. Why?

Why do humans always choose the easiest path? Why do humans always settle for mediocre? Why do we keep conversations light and easy?

I have an answer again. We are lazy and selfish.

Choosing to get to know a person down to their core takes a lot of work. It usually means at least one conversation that goes longer than an hour. It means listening to another person talk for more than ten minutes without interjecting your own experiences and turning the conversation back to yourself. It means asking questions. It means genuinely caring to know what makes another person tick. This isn't easy and most people would elect not to do it. There are paid therapists for that. There are parents for that. Why invest in a person for a couple hours when it may not benefit you at all? The answer to why we don't remains: We are selfish. Lazy.

It is a shame we are so lazy and selfish because there's a great reward to be had in going into someone else's core. Want to know what it is? The reward is, it strengthens your own core. What?! That's right. It really does. All the work you put in to get to someone else's core will actually strengthen your own. Not only do you put in hard work to get there, but once you are there you learn so much more about what to take back to your own core, or what not to take back. You can learn from Granny Smith how she got strong in her faith when she had three miscarriages and lost her husband from cancer. You can learn how your best friend's core was breaking when she was being sexually abused, but repaired when a man of God showed her true love. You can learn so much about how to strengthen your own core from the testimony of others. Get there. Go deeper.

Get personal. Discover cores. It is the most nutritional thing you'll ever do.

I implore you to heed Paul's words from Philippians 2:3-4.

Don't be selfish. Don't try to impress others. Be humble.
Think of others as better than yourselves.
Don't look out for only your own interests,
but take an interest in others too.

Stem

Now before we end this chapter there is one more super cool thing you need to know about your core. Not only does it hold the most nutrients, it's also where the stem connects the fruit to the tree, like an umbilical cord connecting a baby to the life-giving mother. It is the location in which you are sprouting a connection to God. So you can think about it like this: God is the branch and you are the apple. In order to be connected to one another, you need a stem. This stem is created by God and becomes the core of the apple. If the core is neglected or abandoned, the stem breaks and gives way from the branch.

Jesus makes this illustration when he calls himself the True Vine, and we are branches from Him. In John 15:1-17, Jesus takes time to explain to His disciples that if they want to be delicious looking fruit, nutritious and life-giving, then they have to be a part of his vine. There are a lot of trees and vines one can choose to be a part of. Grapes, apples, cherries, kiwis, watermelons, poison ivy, thistles, poison oak, thorn trees, etc. Some choices are good, and some, not so good.

When someone chooses to be a part of God's vine they are choosing the best thing. They are choosing good. They will be a fruit that lives forever and actually provide nutritional value to other people. Their life is a lovely Roscato, a cider, a cherry pie, a fruit salad. What comes out of them is helpful and uplifting to people. They were a fruit of the Spirit. Their life was one of love, joy, peace, patience, kindness, goodness, faithfulness, gentleness and self-control. Their life was well-lived. Their life will have made a difference, big or small. Their life mattered and impacted someone.

Those apart from Christ do not have that luxury. Their life will not be spent wisely. Their life will be followed by hurt, pain, destruction. They will have left oozy, itchy bumps. They gave sores and wounds to others. They cut and poked and picked at people. Anyone who brushed into their company regretted it.

Unfortunately, there is no middle ground. There won't be God's people, then good people, then bad people. There appears to be those on this earth. People who aren't necessarily fruit-bearing but aren't poison ivy either. They're just a plain tree. Just a green vine. Sorry to say, even those aren't good. Anyone apart from Christ is not good. God is the only good thing. If you don't have him, you have nothing good. You simply are, or you're simply bad.

When Jesus encountered a fig tree that was not producing fruit he cursed it (Mark 11:12-25). He commanded it to wither and die because it was not functioning for its intended purpose. It was simply being, taking up space and wasting people's time. Likewise, we are created to bear fruit. We are created to glorify God. That means we do, we go, we love, we obey, we follow. To be a fruitful tree we obey the commandments of Christ. We remain in him. That means we're connected. We're rooted. Established. We're built on the firm Rock. If we aren't, then we're nothing. So just being a "good person," just existing, is not going to cut it either. The only cutting it will do is when you're cut down and cast into the fire. Don't be fooled. There aren't "good people" who don't believe in God that will make it to heaven. Only those connected to the Good God will live forever.

People can be connected to all kinds of things. These days, we're mostly connected to the Internet. If a Verizon tower goes down, if phones aren't permitted on the premises, if there are zero bars, the computer crashes or the satellite can't connect at that moment, some people may straight up go insane. I've seen a perfectly calm person lose their phone and they turn into a nutcase. I've seen teenagers have to hand over their phones in a classroom or a retreat center and break into a sweat and cold chills. It is like they become inoperable without their devices. It is like they are unplugged from the wall of rationale. It can be quite entertaining if you want the truth.

I think it says a whole lot when people turn around and drive miles back to their home when they forget their phone, but won't remember to bring their Bible to church on Sunday. Priorities are way off track in this world. Staying connected to social media is more important than meditating on God's instruction. Online shopping takes more hours of our week than prayer. Talking, face to face, with another one of God's chosen people happens more infrequently than liking posts of people not seen for years. It is like everyone is asking, "Why go to the nations baptizing and teaching when I could stream my favorite show the entire summer?" I ask, "What is the deal, people?"

Fasting

Keeping connected to God may mean unplugging from other things or people. That is the goal behind the Lent season. People are encouraged to give up something for the forty days leading up to Resurrection Sunday. Christ suffered a great deal on Good Friday. He gave his entire life. When we practice Lent we are taking a small part in suffering so we can understand some of what Christ endured. Every year my sister-in-law gives up a plethora of food groups for those 40 days. What she misses most is cheese. Each meal she could be dashing shredded Colby on top of or dipping into Queso, she gets to think about all that Jesus gave up in comparison to her sacrificing a cheese topping. When she hungers for a block of Swiss she can think of the sacrifice of Christ. That is what Lent is supposed to do. It is supposed to realign your connection to Jesus.

The same is true for fasting. The purpose of it is to strengthen your connection with your Provider. As Jesus fasted in the wilderness for 40 days, he had to lean completely on God to strengthen him. He didn't rely on food or water or other people. He was alone with the God who reigns manna from heaven. He had meal times to focus on God instead of finding and cooking food. All his time was given to God. He had no other distractions. His stem was strengthened to the God-Branch.

When we fast we are putting aside the distractions that things we are fasting from can bring. We can fast from more than food. We can fast from technology. We can fast from our television, our refrigerator, our videogames, sugary foods, our phone, talking, alcohol, meat, cigarettes . . . the list goes on and on. Ideally, we fast from something or someone that we know distracts us from spending time with Christ.

People use fasting as a means to hear from God. Throughout Scripture fasting is often done before major decisions are made. In each case people used a time of fasting to clear out distractions and focus on what God was telling them.

I like to imagine fasting this way: Picture a room full of junk. There's furniture, trash, and piles upon piles of boxes. You're on one side of the room and on the other side is God. You can hear each other if you yell over top all the gunk but the view is not clear. You might think you hear him clearly but there's no way to read his lips or hand gestures to be sure of it because you can't see him. So you decide to fast. You want to clear out everything but him. You empty the room. You toss out the chairs, the boxes of baseball cards, sweep the floor of tootsie roll wrappers and tubs of Nutella and you set your phone on the curb outside. When you enter back into the space with God there's nothing between you. You don't have bagels to toast, a screen to stare at or boxes of distractions. It is just you and him. Now is your chance to ask him anything and see his mouth utter the words you thought you heard him say over all the chaos that had once filled the room. That is what fasting is supposed to do.

Purge & Simplify

I don't practice fasting like I should. I'm a pretty good purge-er though. I get urges to suddenly clean my house out from all the junk that builds up. I donate clothes I haven't worn during the year. I toss outdated food. I wipe out the cabinets and clean out drawers. I minimize. I want it cleared out. I want what I need and that is it. I just get sick of seeing stuff. I feel suffocated by all my possessions and I just want it out. So I load up my trunk and I drop off all the meaningless merchandise I had building up in my room and I leave it behind me. It feels good when it is gone. Have you ever had the same urge?

Sometimes purging isn't enough for me. Sometimes I clean my house and my garage and I still feel cramped by it all. Sometimes I just have to get out of it all. So I walk down into my woods or down our little country road. I walk in the fresh open air. I walk through God's nature. I sit under trees on lush grass. I ride my bike so I can be cleaned by the breeze. It refreshes my soul when I get out of all the man-made clutter and find God in the field or the forest. Have you ever done the same?

We all need a good cleansing every now and then. We all get those urges to clean, to throw away, to get away and retreat. We all need space for quiet and peace. God made us this way. He made us with a desire to get back to the simplicity of just being with him. Even extroverts will admit they need sleep and silence. There's just something inside of us that longs to be filled with the right thing or nothing at all. That right thing is God.

You may have heard the idea of a God-shaped hole in your heart. I've heard it said by many pastors in their altar calls. They declare there is a hole in your life that only God can fill. When we try to fill it with other things it is like trying to shove a square peg in a round hole.

The expression comes from a quote by Blaise Pascal's book *Pensees*. He said, "What else does this craving, and this helplessness, proclaim but that there was once in man a true happiness, of which all that now remains is the empty print and trace? This he tries in vain to fill with everything around him, seeking in things that are not there the help he cannot find in those that are, though none can help, since this infinite abyss can be filled only with an infinite and immutable object; in other words by God himself."[6]

This "infinite abyss" inside of us can hold a lot of junk. We can try to fill it with money, furniture, decor from Hobby Lobby, clothes, shoes and purses, but no matter how much we cram inside, it will not be filled. Ask the richest people in the world who do not know God if they are filled with complete satisfaction and I guarantee they won't say yes. Ask the most famous movie stars who don't know God if they have had enough fame and riches and I promise they won't say yes. Ask any money-hungry CEO or daring Youtube-er when enough is enough and they will say never unless they have God. We simply aren't complete humans unless we know him.

Augustine of Hippo wrote in his Confessions, "You have made us for yourself, O Lord, and our hearts are restless until they rest in you."[7]

Restless. We are stir-crazy humans constantly on the run for bigger and better unless we encounter God. Our tanks will always be empty unless we fill up on God. Our hearts are never whole, until filled with Him. Our minds are always wondering until we know God. Our cores are never strong until we are connected to Him.

The first thing a worm will do when they enter an apple is head straight for the core. They are downright determined to get the most nutrients they can with every bite. They know where the good stuff is. Satan operates the same way. He goes straight for the heart of you. He wants to tear down your foundation so when you fall you can't stand back up. I'm telling you the truth. The first thing Satan wants to destroy is what you believe and

---

[6] Pascal, Blaise, 1623-1662. Pascal's Pensées. New York :E.P. Dutton, 1958.

[7] Augustine, of Hippo, Saint, 354-430. The Confessions of Saint Augustine. Mount Vernon :Peter Pauper Press, 19401949.

why you believe it. If he can tear a hole in your morality, in your identity, he will wiggle his fat self in there and rot all the rest of you. Give him an inch and he will take a mile. Once he has you beat on your spiritual front he will conquer the rest of you. You don't stand a chance without your spine.

So I implore you, dear brother-apples and sisters, to heed the words of Isaiah 44:6-8:

> *"This is what the LORD says—*
> *Israel's King and Redeemer, the LORD Almighty:*
> *I am the first and I am the last;*
> *apart from me there is no God.*
> *Who then is like me? Let him proclaim it.*
> *Let him declare and lay out before me*
> *what has happened since I established my ancient*
> *people, and what is yet to come—*
> *Yes, let them foretell what will come.*
> *Do not tremble, do not be afraid.*
> *Did I not proclaim this and foretell it long ago?*
> *You are my witnesses. Is there any God besides me?*
> *No, there is no other Rock; I know not one."*

Don't let Satan fool you. There is no other firm foundation. No other perfect Rock but God alone. He always has been and always will be. Don't let the world fool you. Nothing else will ever satisfy you. Joe Shmoe won't make all your dreams come true. Money won't buy you happiness. Cupcakes won't satisfy your deepest cravings. Jesus will be the first to tell you there is no one good but One, that is God (Mark 10:18). Not one.

Hi, my name is Kamra and I am working on building a strong core and unbreakable stem. I long to be connected to God first and foremost. I want to be a nutritious fruit. I don't want to have to change for people anymore. I want to be the same today and tomorrow at the core of me. I want to say Jesus is my God in the rain and in the sunshine, through the storm and through the calm. I am Kamra "The Rock" Smith because it is on the Rock I stand and it is the Rock who is at my core. Nice to meet you. Now tell me, who are you to your core?

Chapter 7 Reflection

1. Are there basic truths that guide your life and how you live? What are they and how did you adopt them?

2. Your stem is symbolic of what you stay connected to. If someone played the word-association game with you, what would they connect you with?

3. Peter made a statement of faith about Jesus (Matthew 16:16). What is yours?

Jesus forms our identity when He is at our core.

Label the illustration.

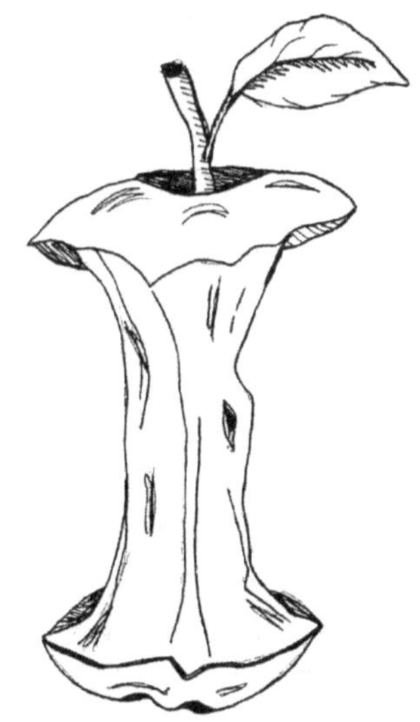

Explain what the core of Christianity should be.

Chapter 7 Challenge

Choose one (Or all three if you're wanting to get toned!) to complete:

1) Choose one of the three challenges from Chapter 1's list of challenges to complete (Purge, Simplify, or Fast).

2. Study John 15:1-17 "The Vine and the Branches." I suggest you: Print it off and mark it up. Highlight, underline, make notes. Ask questions of the passage and use resources to discover the answers. Write it out word for word and try to memorize key verses.

3.A Core Workout.
After each category, write what you believe. I encourage you to include one verse with each answer.

God:
Jesus:
HolySpirit:
Baptism:
Communion:
Other:

Or: Find the "Doctrine of faith" for the Church body you attend. Read it over and see if you agree or disagree. Ask questions to leadership if need be.

If you are doing this study with a small group, make time to discuss this challenge with them and encourage one another.

Chapter 8
Seeds & Soil

Buried within the core of an apple are the seeds. The hard cell of the core frames them in like a protective wall. This is called the Pith. The same substance inside the stem of an apple is what makes up the pith, the plastic-type coating that surrounds the seeds, like marrow within the bone. Therefore, it is a woody material even though it is white or clear. It quite literally is like a wooden wall that protects what is inside. It has to be strong. That is why it was termed "pith." The archaic meaning of the word is "strength, force, vigor." Thus, men of pith are like warriors, strong, courageous, having stamina and muscles. They'd be the ones who surround the King when he is under threat. Likewise, the pith of an apple is a defensive line protecting what is most valuable to the apple - its seeds.

Think of the pith like a treasure chest. Like a wooden box with gold latches and a key. Imagine the container that kept Davey Jones' heart in *The Pirates of the Caribbean, Dead Man's Chest*. Davey Jones kept that key hidden away, but always on his person (beneath his tentacles) because the contents of that chest were of grave importance to him. It was literally his heart! It meant life or death for him. Protecting it was vital.

Well, my friends, you have something within you that is just as important to guard. You have seeds that if properly protected will one day produce new life, give meaning and purpose to your existence. They will leave a legacy. They will be what you can look back on and say, "That is why I was created. That is what I was meant to bring into this world."

Do you ever get jealous of that person who seems to have found their niche? I'm in my thirties and I still don't know what I want to be when I grow up. I've tried a good handful of different jobs. I've got a couple different degrees under my belt but I still shrug, "Is there a career out there for me where I fall into place like a puzzle piece?" When I meet people who are in love with their career or their place in life I wonder how they found it so easily. Like teachers who are passionate about education and could spend all week with those little delinquents. Bless them. Or graphic designers who are excited to get to their computers, artists who dash to their studios, politicians who relish debates - they are so fortunate they get to live to work instead of working to live. These are examples of people who have discovered their seeds.

All of us have different talents and gifts. We all develop seeds unique to ourselves. Apples are the same way. If you were to plant a seed from an apple you bought from the store, it wouldn't produce the exact same kind of apple you took it from. Each seed creates its own kind. In order to have a specific species, you have to graft the tree that seed has sprouted with the kind that already exists. Then, you have to pollinate that tree with the intended species as well. Otherwise, that apple seed will create its own kind of fruit when it grows. You and I are the same. We have unique seeds within us that when planted, create our own kind of species. We have gifts and talents that when orchestrated create our own design. God created us that way.

God is the tree in which we must be grafted with in order for our unique seed to produce a godly fruit. When cross pollinated with Him, we bear the image of the cross. In order for our seeds to produce something that is unique, but still righteous, we make sure we are grafted into the Tree of Life. In order to grow into that which can be grafted into God, we must first recognize our seeds and plant them with care. That begins by recognizing we were created as beings with precious seeds.

God created us purposely and with purpose. We have a function in this life that only we can fulfill. If that weren't true God wouldn't have wasted time creating us. He doesn't create meaningless things that just take up space. He is intentional. He has plans. You, one in the 7.951 billion of us, has a use that no one else can do the same way you were intended to.

Sometimes as I'm writing this book I think I'm saying what hundreds of other authors have probably already said. I doubt I have anything new to add. None of this is revolutionary. Still, I know that while it might be stating the same principles we have heard a hundred times, I'm confident it all is being said in a different way through me, in a way that only I can say it. The vision I was given in the spring of 2023 was unique to me. I saw myself as an apple with a worm. I knew God was painting an illustration for me. For ME. Out of everyone on this planet, he implanted this picture and gave me this message. The combination of my talents has equipped me to foster a seed that was divinely created for me alone.

You too have been given something, or a chunk of things, that if you cultivate it, can grow into something. You have been given passions, talents, skills, education, resources, and if you nurture those things, you will see something come to life. Neglecting those things will keep you stunted, only visible for this lifespan. Jesus warned us of this.

Recorded in Matthew 25:14-30 is the Parable of the Talents. Jesus explained to his disciples that God gave to some servants "talents." This Greek word, τάλαντα (talanta), means a weight or balance of something. To say someone had a talent was to say they had an amount of money. Back then a talent of silver would have been about 6,000 denarii. That is a good chunk of change! That is also why some translations read that when they received their talents, they put their money to work.

But I don't think we need to confine this parable to our money only. God gives us much more than money. He gives us our English definition of talent, which comes from the Greek origin of talanton: a gift, a natural aptitude, skill, a knack. In this parable God is giving gifts to his servants. He is blessing them with something. He encourages them to use what he has freely given them to expand his kingdom. You can read in the parable that some of the servants did exactly that. They invested their money. They went to work. They cultivated their seeds. When they did this they saw results. They saw the expansion of God's kingdom. Their money grew from some to a lot. Their talents produced good works. Their gifts blessed others. The one who elected to keep their talent to themselves was yelled at. "You selfish, lazy slave! Why didn't you share? Why didn't you scatter?" All that he was given wouldn't ever be used to bring new life, power to the powerless, hope to the hopeless, meaning to the trivial days. It was squandered and the seed would die with him.

Jesus gave this parable as a warning and an encouragement. He gave it as a lesson to be learned about God's kingdom. If we want to be someone who leaves a mark on this earth, who can be looked back upon by others and then say, "They really used all they had for God's glory," then we have to discover and put our seeds to the soil. We have to acknowledge God has given us "talents" and we must put them to work.

It is time for some self-evaluation. I want you to ask yourself what you are good at. I want you to make a list of talents you have. I want you to answer, "What makes me unique and different from others?" I want you to truly think about what God has given you. Take stock of what you have in your bank account. Look at what you have stored in your home, barns, garages and attics. What can you make, bake, cook, grow, do? Where are you? Who is around you? What are the needs in your community? What is missing in your church ministry?

Ask all the questions. Then start connecting the dots. Do you paint, draw, sculpt? Could any of those mediums display God's glory? Do you sing, speak in public, teach, write poems? I bet all those talents could highlight your Maker.

When those connections are made and acted upon, guess what you've done: You have discovered a seed within you that can produce one heck of a tree!

If you're thinking your talent is too tiny or wimpy, trivial or even stupid, I want to stop you right there. No such thing. It can't be. It isn't. In this parable of the talents, one servant was given five and another was given two but when both of them used what they had when asked, God was happy. He let both of them enter into his joy. He called them "good and faithful" and he blessed them. He grew things out of them. He took their seeds and made trees.

Whether you have five or two, God has given to you. Whether your talent is Mozart-piano-level-skills or Mary Had a Little Lamb level, if you use it to make God happy, he will grow something beautiful out of it. If you have five dollars compared to someone else's five million, he can still grow a magnificent tree from that if you invest it deeply into God's hands.

You, with your seeds seeming so tiny and minute, can become a great space for God's kingdom work to be done. This is what Jesus demonstrated in his parable of the mustard seed. Recorded in Matthew 13:31-32, Jesus explains God's kingdom is like when a tiny mustard seed gets planted and grows into a great garden tree that houses birds far and near.

While this parable can paint a really broad picture, let me take it down to scale for the seed illustration I'm trying to get you to understand here. Your seed, that passion you have for running, your unexplained love for law enforcement, your basket-weaving skill, you knack with children, that hankering you have to end sex-trafficking, your capacity to listen to people hours on end, your aptitude for music, how you picked up a guitar and knew how to play in five minutes, that weird desire to get to Kenya when you've never been, all these seeds you believe to be miniscule, were given to you for a reason. If you invest in them, take time to plant them in the right resources, the right people, the right places, I guarantee they can grow into something so large and meaningful in your life that you and others will step back and say, "That grew into that?!"

I'll give you an example. My friend Matt is from a small town like me. He's from a family of farmers, just like me. But as he got older and he married a beautiful woman, he discovered a seed in him for adoption. A desire was nestled inside his core to bring home children from Liberia, Africa. How it got there, I'm sure he was just as perplexed as the next person. But he and his wife went for it. Fast forward through their faith journey and you'll discover their seed for adoption grew into a tree called Psalm 82:3 Mission.[8] This is a fifty acre plot of land in Liberia that now has four foster homes, a school, a medical clinic, a church, a soccer field, a playground, wells with clean water, agriculture, chickens and goats, and more to come. Liberian adults are staffed, able to provide for families and fill their bellies. Liberian children are cared for, fed, educated and shown the love of Christ. Communities surrounding this mission site are cared for, fed, educated, and brought into the family of Christ. One man and one woman were given a seed for adoption and when they entrusted it to God, taking action, it grew into a tree where many Liberian birds come to nest and find rest in its branches. See what I mean?

You and I are no different in our ability to be used for God's kingdom. We all, no matter how small the town we are from, no matter how poor the farmers and smelling of manure, we can be used in mighty ways and do mighty things through Christ Jesus our Lord. After all, God has a knack for using the most unlikely. He used an old man and barren woman to birth his Israelite nation. He gave the lying, stealing, manipulating Jacob the dream of His ladder. He gave David the talent of writing poems so we have bundles of powerful Psalms. He also gave David the skill of using a slingshot. Does that sound like a big and powerful seed? But when David used it to bring God glory, it took down Goliath and a battle was won for God's kingdom. That's how he used one shepherd. He'd go on to appear first to more lowly shepherds when his birth was announced. He used the talents of fishermen to make disciples. He used an adulterous woman to reach Samaria. And the list could

---

[8] Psalm 82:3 Mission, Inc. (2022) psalm823.org

go on and on. But let's turn to the author of two thirds of the New Testament who was once a murderer.

Saul was reinstated as Paul when Jesus encountered him on the road to Damascus. God gave that man talents to use for the building of his Church. When Paul realized he was given this special seed, he went to work planting it. In turn, he reached the Gentiles. He changed nations. His tiny speck of a mustard seed became a nation-bearing tree. This is the man who cried, "I am the worst of all sinners" (1 Timothy 1:15). Don't you see? If God can use this man, who believed himself to be the absolute worst, can't he use you and I? Can't he plant tiny seeds within us that can grow into marvelous things? I tell you, HE CAN.

More so, God WANTS to. Have you ever thought of it like that? That God wants to use you for a special purpose? The fact that he knows every hair on your head and personally knitted you together in your mother's womb tells me that when he created each of us he did it with intentionality. He gave me the gift of writing for a reason. He gave you the gift of singing for a reason. To that guy he gave strength. To that girl he gave a steady hand. For my dad, he gifted him with a guitar. For my mom, the ability to bake the perfect pie. For my Grandma, a green thumb. This list could go on and on. Each person was designed with these seeds inside just waiting to come out and make great things on this earth for God's glory.

One thing I love most is discovering what people's seeds are. As we discussed in the previous chapter on "Core," a deep conversation can take you into the heart of a person. There, in the center, lies these beautiful treasures waiting to be freed from the chest. You catch glimmers of them when the person's eyes light up when they hit the topic. You see a smile spread across their face. They sit up a little straighter. They start talking a little faster. They spill open when a passion is discovered. It is such a beautiful thing to see unfold. Sometimes, they didn't even know it was a seed until it was unearthed. You dig long enough and a dream or a memory pops up from childhood. Soon, they are starting to remember how great it was. They start to feel fire inside. They can even get teary-eyed and emotional.

I saw it happen one day as my friend sat on the couch trying to explain why she felt discontent and out of place at her seemingly perfect job. She couldn't put her finger on it but something was just . . . missing. Eventually she remembered a passion she once had as a child. She had a love for law enforcement. Many things in her life had pointed to that forgotten passion. She had forgotten it, but suddenly it was there again. A seed.

Discovering your seeds can turn your life around. It can make a path appear. It can make a mission mandatory. It gives drive. It fuels reason. It makes a career a hobby. It takes living into thriving. It gives a dying person the motivation to live.

One of the saddest things to see is a person who has had their seed stolen or let it die. They once were passionate about a subject, but went cold. They once felt fire in their bones to speak and debate, but fizzled out. They had a dream, but it died. They had a vision but it got lost in the chaos. They were told they'd never amount to anything, to toss their seeds to the wind. They tried to grow that master plan that budded in their imagination but it was unapproved by the Bank, or was ridiculed by the public. When you see someone like this, they are empty inside. They have nothing in them to live for. They just get through each day, going to that job they hate then sitting on their couch at home. They don't talk about what-if's and could-be's. They live stuck in the have-to's.

This is exactly where Satan wants people. He heads straight into that core and snatches up any seeds he can find. He doesn't want people living their best lives. He doesn't want people living at all. He wants them in Hell, on earth and ever after. Satan will come after your passions and dreams. He will come after your kids. He will come after your organization, your mission, your plan, your vision, and he will even try to corrupt your talents. When he's got your seeds, he's got you on the deathbed. Be on guard, Christian. Be men and women of pith or be men and women raped of hope and purpose.

We don't always know what our seeds will become. My friend doesn't know where her love of law enforcement will take her. Maybe she will be a dispatcher, an officer, an FBI agent, a psychological profiler, or a sergeant in the Army. Maybe she will start her own non-profit. Who knows what will happen with it, but I guarantee if it is planted in the right soil, it will matter in God's kingdom.

Soil

Everyone has talents and gifts. A lot of people can dance and sing. A lot can paint and some can sew. Others can bake, teach, speak, debate, etc. Some people use these things for good, some don't use them at all, and some use them for bad. One person can take the gift of teaching and instruct someone how to read and write. Another can use their gift of teaching to instruct others how to curse and inflict harm. A skilled public speaker can be motivational or cultic. It is a tragic dilemma but it is real. As mentioned above, we must make sure we graft our seeds into the Cross. We also need to make sure we plant our seed in the proper soil.

There is only one soil that will produce the best vegetation: The Word of God. Jesus explains this in his Parable of the Sower recorded in Matthew 13:1-23. The seed in this case was the person. God, as the sower, scatters his people among all kinds of soil in this world. So again, this parable can be broader in context but let me connect it to the seed illustration I am trying to explain here.

Jesus describes various types of soil - a path, rocky ground, thorny ground, or good soil. Let's go through them one by one.

The Path Soil

Some try to root in paths where the Enemy comes along and can easily pluck them up. This is like a person who wants to implement their plans in a chaotic atmosphere, or right in the middle of temptation. It obviously isn't going to thrive there. There's too much traffic. There are too many people ready to step on your idea, your passions, and kick you into the gutter. It is as if this person wants to be in harm's way. They could just hand their seeds over to Satan and say, "Here you go. I don't plan on doing anything with this life anyway. Just kill me." They see their seed and think it is worthless so they aren't going to search for good soil. They take for granted what they have been given. Seeds planted in this soil will die and that person will never see their passions or talents flourish into the beautiful thing it could have been.

The Rocky Ground

Some people try to grow where rocks wreck the landscaping. They invest in people and places that only let them go so deep. Their passions and visions can't reach max capacity because they are caught between a rock and hard place. There are people who won't budge in this life. They can listen to you burst with pride about your idea but if it means they have to move an inch, they'll tell you no. Some people are just dying to make their idea come to life. They are bursting at the seams to use their talents. But they are in a soil that won't let them root. It is all talk and no support. If seeds are sewn here they are doomed to stay as small, weak, little creatures that won't last the haul long. It will be visions that quickly die. Passions that quickly fade and talents that are lost over time.

The Thorny Ground

The person who tries to grow their seed in thorny ground is the one who gets distracted by all the other plants growing around them and eventually gets choked out. Some people know they have a great skill and a wonderful idea, so they plant it. They love it and they want it to grow but they also really love their neighbor's, and their cousin's, and their boss', and that one guy's, and that one girl's. Before long they are trying to grow in another direction and spread over yonder and up the hill. They get tangled in other people's ideas and visions. Other people start to spread into their zone. They climb over top of them and smother their passions. They want to transform what was meant to grow so beautifully into a thorny mess. They want to kill you so they have more space to grow themselves. Seeds planted in this soil will either die or be used to hold up a much more ugly and prickly being.

The Good Soil

This person knows good soil from bad. This person knows the value of their seed. They know it is precious. They know it needs the right conditions in order to thrive. They know hard work must go into the soil in order for it to have the best results. They note where they need more and where they need less. They make changes and desire righteousness. This person puts in the research for their talents, gifts and skills to be most fruitful. They don't invest in any old person or any old place. They recognize who will be good company and what will benefit them. How do they know? They test the soil against the Word of God.

We have soil samples taken from the farm every year. A man comes with a pointy rod and shoves it in the dirt about twenty times in various fields. He takes it back to his lab where he tests it to see how much pH is in the dirt. Based on that he can tell us if we need more fertilizer, more lime, etc. If we follow his instructions and invest money, machinery, materials and time into making our soil healthier, we get more bountiful crops.

Let's apply this logic to your apple-life. You have precious seeds within you. You need to plant these in the best possible soil you can if you want to have the best results. So first you need to understand what good soil is so you know what to look for. Jesus clarifies that the good soil is his Word. Anything good comes from this. Imagine your Bible lying open face up in your yard. Everything that grows out of it will be beautiful, nutritious, strong and just plain good. So now you lie down in your yard facing up. Imagine things growing out of you. Is it good, nutritious and beautiful, or destructive, ugly and dark? If it is the latter, then you aren't mirroring the Word.

If you want good things to grow from your seeds, you need to plant them in what mirrors the Word. You need to invest your talents and skills, your visions and passions in that which matches the Word of God. You won't be able to do this if you don't first recognize what the Word is. That means you actually have to read it. Then when others quote it or bash it, you can have a standard in which to test them against. That is a very important practice to have in your life. You have to test the soil to make sure it is like Jesus.

John, a disciple of Jesus, reminded his readers there are a lot of spirits around, some are bad and some are good. If we want to know which is which we have to test them.

"Do not believe every spirit, but test the spirits to see
whether they are from God,
for there are many false ones in this world" (1 John 4:1).
So how do we test them? In the soil-sampling world, the elements within the soil can be tested by dropping a liquidized portion of the dirt onto a paper strip. That's my unscientific way of putting it anyway. This paper begins to change colors according to the chemical reaction. The color change is revealing what components are within. In other words, the soil's true colors come to life.

When someone is tested, their true colors come to life as well. You can see what is really buried within people when you give them enough time. You can see if there is consistency in their color, so to speak. You can see if they shift when others are around. You can see if they accept one verse in the Bible but not another. Some people adapt like a chameleon.

This goes back to what I was referencing in the skin chapter. A mature and Holy Spirit-filled Christian ought to have a solid color rounding their apple-body. The Holy Spirit doesn't change. He is God. He is the same yesterday, today and tomorrow. His paper test would prove the same color in every situation, every day. From Genesis to Revelation, the paper is the same color. The Spirit is the same.

When a person is filled with the Holy Spirit they ought to be consistent in color all their days. They ought to match the coloring of the Word. They are black and white. They are bright, not dull or hidden under bowls. They stand out. They are peculiar.

Do you know what it means to be peculiar? It means when our soil is tested, we reveal a color unlike anyone else in the world. We are striking. We are unique. We are uncharacteristic. If the whole world were to be tested there would be a common theme. There would be a general rule. A standard. Most people are this hue, perhaps even dark. But when Christians are tested, they should shoot out of the ordinary. That is how Jesus was. He stood out. He was different. His followers got identity changes. They went from one life to the next. Their soil that once tested so completely bland and featureless transformed to a striking experience. No wonder Jesus started calling James and John the Brothers of Thunder. They went from blah to BAM. The disciples of Jesus went from fitting in like a chameleon to standing out in the crowd. No more adapting. No more conforming. They were radiant.

When we test the soil of others we get to the core of them. We see where their true loyalty lies. We see who their god is. When hard times come, we see where they run. When pressured, we see if they change. You know what I'm talking about. You've figured out who your true friends are. You entrusted them with a secret and they kept it. That's a true friend. Or how about that one you thought was your real friend until you found out they gossiped about you behind your back and started awful rumors. Their true colors came out. They aren't really your friend.

I've heard people say you know when you have a best friend if they show up to help you move or drive you to the airport. A best friend doesn't just say they will help you pack. They are the ones who show up with the pickup truck. They're the ones who wait at the terminal. And I'd like to add: Real friends know your true colors.

In the movie *Trolls,* Branch sings a song to his downtrodden friend, Poppy. The queen troll had finally given up. Her usual happy-go-lucky personality disappeared. She had lost hope that she could rescue her troll friends. She no longer believed in herself. As a result, her vibrant pink hair and colorful clothes faded to black and white. Branch stepped forward and delivered the lyrics of Cyndi Lauper from a song called "*True Colors.*"

If this world makes you crazy
And you've taken all you can bear
You call me up
Because you know I'll be there
And I'll see your true colors
Shining through
I see your true colors
And that's why I love you
So don't be afraid to let it show

Branch lifted Poppy's spirit and the color came back to her cheeks. She perked up and was once again her joyful and optimistic self. They would go on to save the rest of her troll friends from the Bergens.

Why did I divert to this scene from a children's movie, you may ask? That scene really showed a friend stepping up. He called Poppy out of her darkness and back into the light. He was basically saying (or singing), "This is not who you really are, Poppy. You have the light. Shine it." What a good friend.

If you and I want to be good friends too, we must help our friends stay true to the color of Christ. He is light. He is bright. When you see them dimming or trying to hide, encourage them to shine. When you see them worrying, falling into depression, go to them and share your light. You can sing over them words from Bethel's song The Light in You.

When you discover your seed you're going to want to make sure you plant it in good soil. You're going to want to make sure you have genuine friends. When they hear your seed-story, they won't laugh and tell you to put it where the sun doesn't shine. Planting around the wrong people can make or break your seed, can stunt your growth or kill you.

Likewise, planting your seed in the soil of a bad spirit will end you. Unfortunately, Satan has found ways to make his soil look oh so good. He spruces it up with fancy looking landscaping rock, birdbaths and feeders, but beneath the surface a worm infestation is eating up roots and devouring cores. Those flashy beings and fancy things will fade away. They won't last. Their seeds are chewed up and spat out by demons. Don't be fooled, brother and sister, his soil is poison.

In case I've lost you in all this soil-sampling lingo and the three parables of Jesus, this is what I'm trying to say: The seeds within you are treasures and so they need the best soil you can give them. In other words, your dreams, talents, passions, and visions the Lord has put in you are unique, special and must be planted! These things will produce the best results if they are entrusted to the Lord and always kept in hands. They are best taken care of in the company of friends who keep you in the Light, as a bright color. The motivation needs to come from the Word. The intention must be to glorify the Creator. If so, those seeds will grow into something great.

Hi, my name is Kamra and I have seeds the Enemy wants to devour. I have dreams I want to see come true. I have visions I need to put on paper. I have talents wanting to display the greatness of God. I can't let the Enemy steal them. I can't put these seeds where they will never grow, where they will be taken advantage of, stolen or discouraged. I need to plant these seeds in God's Good Soil. I don't want them to die inside of me without ever taking root. I want to be a good and faithful servant to all that which God has given me. How about you?

Chapter 8 Reflection

1. A seed can be recognized as something special within you that, if invested in others, all can see growing. What is something growing out of you? If you aren't sure, ask others what they see coming from you. If you are afraid the answer is nothing, what seed is in you that is ready to be planted?

2. What kind of people did God use in the Bible to grow great things out of? Give examples.
In what way are you like those people?

3. Think of people outside of Scripture who have done great things with what they had for God's glory. It can be someone you know personally, like a parent, or someone you've heard about. Who are they and how were they successful? What can you learn from them? Label the illustration. What are your seeds?

Chapter 8 Challenge

Choose one (Or all three if you're on fire!) to complete:

1) Discover your seeds through self-evaluation.

- Your talents:
- Your spiritual gifts:
- Things you are passionate about:
- What is unique about you?
- Where are you (place, setting, season)?
- Who surrounds you?
- Your Dreams / Visions / Goals:
- How can you use this for God's glory?

2) Test your soil.

- What color would you use to describe you?
- What color would others use to describe you?
- Are you mirroring the Word of God?
- Are you encouraged by your friends and family to thrive for Christ?
- Are there people choking you out?

3) A true friend knows your true colors and shows you theirs (which ought to be the light and bright color of Christ). Name them, then personally thank them for their friendship (through a note, text, call, email, lunch or coffee date, etc.).

If you are doing this study with a small group, make time to discuss this challenge with them and encourage one another.

Chapter 9
The Good Farmer's Orchard

I had the displeasure of writing a chapter about
The Worm and another about Worms, but this chapter . .
. oh this wonderful chapter has finally come. You've
pushed through chapters on soft spots and bruises.
You've read so much on how to be the best apple you
can be - staying strong in the core, connected with a firm
stem and treasuring your seeds. On top of all of that you
had to keep in mind that an army of worms wants to
destroy it all. It all may not have sounded as simple as it
started in chapter one where you learned your purpose
in life was to hang in the presence of God and enjoy him
forever. So now I get to take it all back to home plate. It
is all going to come full circle here. Hopefully, by the end,
you'll see your purpose is still achievable because you
have the Great Farmer and His pesticides.

The Wild

Last year we had a rogue pumpkin patch pop up
in the pasture. I had thrown the previous year's old
pumpkins into the lot for the cows to munch on.
Apparently they hadn't eaten all the seeds and some
took root. A year after the tossing a wild patch had
sprung up. They didn't produce many pumpkins and
when they did the cows quickly squashed them under
hoofs. They were far from home, far from a water hose,
a tiller, my hoe . . . They weren't in the right place. The
pumpkins were not under my care and so they produced
poorly. I got to hand it to them - they tried. They reached
their yellow flowers as high above the hay as they could,

but they didn't stand a chance there. Most wild things don't.

Wild things are that which are untamed, uncultivated, exposed to the natural environment. They are things that don't follow direction and have no leader. They are things that fend for themselves and play the game, "survival of the fittest." For this reason, wild things are usually fierce and feral.

I've had my fair share of encountering wild creatures. It is a continuous battle against some of the wild things that want to torment the domesticated. In one summer we trapped and disposed of 13 critters trying to get into our chicken coup - mainly raccoons and possums. But there are so many others that pose a danger to our sweet hens. There are foxes, coyotes, snakes, and even an occasional wild dog. Two summers ago our family dog, Cookie, had to help me chase a wild dog off the farm that successfully killed four chickens and harmed multiple others in just minutes.

The battle for survival is for more than our farm animals. I also have to fend for my plants. Rabbits, deer and all sorts of furry critters like moles and squirrels love to have field days in my mulch. For some reason my hostas taste better than wild clover to bunnies and my ornamental trees feel better for deer to rub their antlers against. Coons like my garden corn and slugs will come for miles to taste my flowers. The amount of cages I have in my yard to protect my gardens appears I am imprisoning all my plants. But it is for their own protection, trust me.

You see there is a drastic difference between a wild creature and a tame one. Take the rose bush for example. My tame ones that get manicured and are tender and bursting with roses laced in delicate petals. On the other hand, the one rose bush that has decided to go wild has developed giant thorns on it that gash my fingers if I try to touch it. The roses on it are pathetic but the spikes are enormous!

When something goes wild it develops features that it believes will protect it. A wild dog will bite and attack whatever is moving so that it can get some foot. My calm and collected Cookie, on the other hand, will try to lay in my lap for a treat. My dog doesn't have wild features because it has grown up knowing she has someone that wants to take care of her. She doesn't have to fend for herself. She has me, her trainer.

The point I am trying to make with all this is: Wild things don't have a trainer. They don't have direction. They pop up in places without a purpose and just try to survive. Their life is hard and marked by privation. Because of this, they will be rough and pricklier than usual. They will develop characteristics that keep others back so harm stays an arm's length away. Therefore, they will be alone. They will be that one dandelion that tries to make it in the sidewalk crack. They will be the wild dog on the run, with no best friend and no bowl of food waiting on the front porch. They will be the rose bush that thistles and stabs.

People who refuse to heed direction will be a wild bunch. As a former Elementary teacher, I tell you this is a true statement! We operate better when there are rules and parameters. Things go much more smoothly if there is a syllabi or an outline. We crave structure. We love organization! Okay, maybe not all of us, but I believe we apple-humans were created with a desire to be cared for. We have a longing to be protected, guided and assured. We feel better when we have that.

Guess what . . . There is a person who wants to give you exactly that. He wants to take care of you and

make sure you are protected. He wants to guide you,
lead you, assure you and encourage you. He wants to
tend to you like a fragile flower. He wants to prune and
trim you so you grow into a wonderful little tree. He's a
good gardener like that. He's a loving father like that.
And to make my point perfectly clear: He's a great
farmer like that.

Farmer God

God is the planter, grower and sustainer of all
things that are under his care. Unfortunately, not every
one of us apple-humans wants to be under His care. For
some, the looks of the wild are more appealing than that
of the well-tended orchard. Some of us gaze upon the
patch of wild flowers and believe it must be a space of
care-free bliss where plants can do whatever they want,
wherever and however. From a distance it may look like
a zone where worries don't exist, rules aren't needed
and everyone lives in harmony just minding their own
bees. But that is exactly what Satan wants it to look like
from a distance. He wants to draw people into his little
garden space with the belief that everyone is happier
when all things are relative. What he keeps hidden are
the pesky worms, the thorns, the poison, and the reality
that when you are there you are all alone, defenseless
and exposed to evil.

I can relate to people who think the other side,
the one without God, must be an easier and more
pleasurable life. I grew up in the manicured garden-life of
Christianity. I had a lot of guidance and rules. I had a lot
of structure and support. In 2023, however, I wondered if
a life without may be easier. I wondered if I could toss
out God and all that I felt he required of me in exchange
for a life of just trying to make myself "happy." I was

surrounded by people who didn't believe in God. They told me that their life was easier than mine because they didn't have to care about other people or what God said was right or wrong. So, I bought into it. I ventured to their side where I thought being a wildflower would be easier than a tame one.

Can I be honest with you? For a little bit, it was fun. I felt "free" in a way. Then, just as quickly as it was fun, it became deadly. I felt suffocated under thorns. I felt overpowered by poisonous vines. I started to fear I was going to be smothered by the chaos of it all. I could shout and scream but I felt too far from anyone to hear me, as if I was in the middle of a deep wood where only wild things live. There was no good gardener to weed me out some space. Worry, fear, anxiety and depression grew like massive trees all around me. Trying to get a little bit of sunlight meant I had to bend and contort for even a smidgen of warmth. I was hidden beneath branches that kept me in their shade. I learned really fast that I wasn't going to thrive there. I was in danger there.

It is sad we apple-humans believe we have to experience the wild side of life in order to really understand how good we have it in God's garden. I can't tell you how much I regret some of what I did and went through in 2023. Sure, I am stronger for it and have learned a lot from it, but I still wish I could say I had done that without having made the mistake of leaving God to learn it. As the saying goes, "A smart person learns from their mistakes, but a wise person learns from the mistakes of others." This is true for what I'm trying to say. I wish I had listened to the caution that was given to me for years, "The grass always looks greener on the other side." But I didn't listen. I wasn't wise.

Don't be stupid, my sweet reader-friend. If you want to be wise, learn from my testimony and HEED

THE WORD OF GOD. He has given you the Holy Bible to guide and instruct you. His Word is a lamp for your feet and a light for your path (Psalm 119:105). While it may appear to be a whole lot of rules, the instructions therein are more like a love letter from a God who wants to keep you close to him because he wants to keep you safe. He longs to be with you. He created you for that very reason. He created you so you could enjoy each other.

All the time God wants to spend with you is not so he can turn you into a garden statue. God is not in the business of making you stiff, rigid, unmovable, and robotic. He isn't creating a bunch of garden gnomes. He has created us as living, breathing beings. He wants us to be expressive and creative. He loves the uniqueness of each of us. That is why he knows every hair on our head (Luke 12:7). He wouldn't waste his time creating us so uniquely - with our own eye and hair color, shoe size, belly button depth, earlobe shape, personality, talents, gifts, dreams and passions - if he didn't intend to keep you exclusively you and his. I told you in the seeds chapter and I'll tell you here again: You are special and there is no one else like you.

His Orchard

In God's orchard there are all types of species. His orchard is vast, but his orchard is also purposeful. There isn't one fruit that is unchecked. He keeps an eye on everyone. He is the type of farmer who will walk through his garden everyday just to be in the presence of his creation. It has been that way since the beginning.

Prior to the Fall, Adam and Eve were in close proximity to their Creator every day. I suspect they went for daily walks where they talked about everything they did while apart. But when they ate of the fruit that Satan had tempted them into tasting, they became ashamed people and hid from God. Let's take a look at the text:

Then the man and his wife heard the sound of the LORD God as he was walking in the garden in the breezy time of the day, and they hid from the LORD God among the trees of the garden.
But the LORD God called to the man, "Where are you?"
He answered, "I heard you in the garden, and I was afraid because I was naked; so I hid."
Genesis 3:8-10

Prior to the pesky worm coming and tripping Adam and Eve up, these two were walking and talking with God in the perfect Garden of Eden. They were in a space God had intended them to be. Under his supervision they were taken care of. They didn't have to worry about what to eat or drink or what to wear. They were carefree and enjoying the breezy time of every day. As soon as they were out of it, however, they were wearing uncomfortable and itchy fig leaves. They were separating themselves. They were distant. They were ashamed. The life the Tempter had been promising was a lie. At the time it sounded like a good idea, but when they entered it they quickly learned it was a place of death. That place is not what God intended us to live in.

God created an orchard that is a space of freedom and enjoyment. I know we can look out at the wild patches and think they are the ones who are truly free but it is actually under the care of a Great Farmer that we are in a space of ease. That's why Paul said,

"Where the Spirit of the Lord is, there is freedom"
(2 Corinthians 3:17).

Think back to that rogue pumpkin patch I told you about. They certainly appeared carefree just popping up where they like, their vines running atop manure, but they were actually a doomed patch where they lay. They had no shot at success. They were trampled by cows much bigger than them. They didn't get water unless the sky poured it out. They didn't have a terrace to climb so their flowers could soak up the sun instead of being hidden in hay. If they had been in my garden they would have favored much nicer.

The same is true for you and I. When we are under the Good Farmer God's care, we are not restrained from freedom, we are protected from evil and given what we need so we can grow with blissful creativity. Under His protection we are bound to grow to max capacity. We are certain to bust at the stems with mounds of beauty. When we take his instruction, his manicuring, his pruning of scraggly branches, his fertilizing and watering, we are going to prosper.

Life apart from him will be itchy, difficult, uncomfortable and shameful, but on the flip side, being pruned doesn't sound like too much fun, does it? It is the action of cutting away or trimming a part of something so that another part can grow. As someone who has literally had the tip of their finger cut off, pruning has a negative connotation. Yet, if you are a gardener or farmer you may know the benefit of what a good and routine pruning can do. Certain plants, like roses, need pruned every spring or every fall and sometimes during both seasons. Some plants need to be topped and suckered, like tobacco. Some trees, like the apple, need branches cut out so more sun can reach the center of the tree to grow larger and more evenly balanced fruits throughout. Goats need their hooves trimmed. Horses do too. Your kid's hair even needs a good trimming every now and then. I could go on and on . . .

Pruning and trimming is for your betterment. God regulates you so that you can grow more successfully and enjoy life more fully, not so that he can harm or control you. I think of it like when my mom would have to trim my bangs. If left uncut, my bangs would get long enough to cover my eyes. When they would I was constantly blowing them out of my face, tossing my hair like I had a twitch or forcing myself to work one-handed while one held my hair out of my face. I needed mom to trim my bangs so I could see better and work more efficiently. In the same way, God is in the business of cutting away that which prohibits you from seeing him clearly.

I'll never forget the reaction I had from a teenage boy when I was teaching about the Creation and Fall account in youth group. When we learned about the Tree of the Knowledge of Good and Evil, Camden spoke up: "Why didn't Adam and Eve just cut that tree down when they learned God didn't want them to eat from it?" Doing so may have saved us a whole lot of trouble if they had. Camden was right. Why didn't Adam fix up an ax and take to hacking? If he had cut it away, maybe he wouldn't have been hiding in bushes and running from God.

We ought to ask ourselves a similar question now: What is in my life that should just be cut away so it won't hinder me from following God? The Good Farmer knows what those things are. He wants to cut them away. If you're wondering what they could be take a look at the advice of Jesus (Matthew 5:29-30):

If your right eye causes you to stumble,
gouge it out and throw it away.
It is better for you to lose one part of your body than for
your whole body to be thrown into hell. And if your right
hand causes you to stumble, cut it off and throw it away.
It is better for you to lose one part of your body than for
your whole body to go into hell.

Before you start hyperventilating, hear me out. You do not literally need to poke out your eyeballs and saw off your hands. I think God would rather use those body parts to build his kingdom than for them to become doggy treats. No, you don't literally need to do that, but you do figuratively. You need to examine what in your life is causing you to sin and you need to cut that sin out of your life. Nah, you need to let God cut that sin out of your life. Let the Good Farmer do his work. Let him remove from you that which has been blocking your view of the Saving Son.

When God prunes he is doing it so that better things can grow in its removal. Jesus stated:

"I am the vine and my Father is the gardener.
He cuts away every branch that does not bear fruit in
me. He prunes every branch that bears fruit so that it will
bear more fruit." John 15:1-3

Pruning happens even to those who are being Christ-like. Things will get taken away, but it isn't so that God can replace it with nothing. It isn't so that he can get his kicks in harming you and seeing you bleed. It is done so new things can grow, or more! I do the same thing with my blackberry vines every year. I cut away the dead ones from the previous season so more nutrients can flow directly to the new shoots and even more blackberries will produce. So take heart. Pruning is painful, but it is worth it. Rejoice through it, my friend. Better and more abundant things are going to replace it.

This orchard that you get to be a part of is not one where each plant has to follow so many rules and do many good deeds in order to be beautiful and stay put. No, this orchard is one where plants get to come and be cared for by a Good Farmer God. They don't do the work that makes them grow so beautifully. They simply get to take the advice of the Good Farmer. What he says needs pruned, they let him prune. When he says they need more sun and less water, they nod in agreement. Where he says they should climb, they happily go. Since they know they will be their most beautiful and happiest selves if they do what he says, they joyfully obey.

It is the greatest honor to be a part of God's orchard. In his garden everyone has their own space and purpose. They get their own special container. They get the type of mulch that will best support them. They get to be surrounded by what is healthy for them. They even get pesticides.

Pesticides

Pesticides help manage pests. Since there are many types of pests for a plant, there are many types of pesticides. Specifically, there are herbicides which help control weeds. There are fungicides that help control fungi and the pollination processes between female and male plants. And while there are more with purposes that are hard for me to explain, there is one other that I think we will find particularly useful: Insecticides. These help manage insects.

While a worm is not classified as an insect, a moth is. If you recall from previous chapters, the Codling Moth Caterpillar is the nemesis we have narrowed in on for our apple-lives. It is the creature that lays eggs that develop into grubby little worms that eat their way through apples that grow into moths that eventually lay their own legs, and so the cycle continues. Those guys. Those nasty little larva that lurk on branches just inching towards fruits to devour. Remember them?

An insecticide traditionally gets sprayed by a farmer through a hose that is hooked up to a tank where the juices of destruction are housed. The liquid mists onto branches, leaves and flowers, where it is absorbed by what it lands on. It is most successful at killing eggs and bugs who suck in the vapors. The little tormentors die on the spot and fall to the ground if they are sprayed. If by chance a bug comes along that was not sprayed, they still run the risk of dying if they bite into a plant that has absorbed the insecticide. For example, a worm who was clear of the spraying may decide to venture up a tree and approach the fruit. If that fruit was sprayed it has a protective barrier. When the worm bites into it, it will absorb the insecticide and die.

I know everyone feels differently about chemicals being sprayed onto their foods. I won't even attempt to go there. Let's not get hung up on that right now. Let me get you to the point I am trying to make. God has given us insecticides to fight off the worms of our apple-lives.

Here is what God sprays on us for protection:
His Word (Genesis through Revelation)
His Spirit (Omnipresent and Omniscient)
His Son (the Perfect Example & Sacrifice)
His Power (Omnipotent)
His Body (The Church that builds one another up)

God is always ready to spray the demons inching their way toward you if one happens to get into his Garden. He always tries to keep you from harm by killing any evil thing that may have been laid on your branch. He doesn't want these things in his presence. He doesn't want them to separate you from Him. But he has given you free-will to roll into whatever orchard you want. He has given you a choice to accept his protection or not. He knows what is best for you but he can't force you to climb terraces or grow towards the Son.

Right now you have some insecticide laying at your bedside. It is leather bound and printed in nearly every language. **The Word** is available to you. God is ready to spray you with it if only you'd open it up and face him. Crack open the text and pray, "Word of God, please nurture my soul. Speak to me. Spray my Enemy."

The Spirit is always willing to guide you. He knows what is in your heart. He knows the longing of your soul. He knows everything and he is always around. Why do we elect to ignore him? It is as if we know the insecticide is right there but we let the worms inch closer than He. Open up your heart and mind. Let him groan. Let him lead.

Jesus is another incredible resource we forget. We forget that within the Bible is a recording of things he did, things he said. It is there that we may copy it. It is there that we may accept what he said and what he did. That means we accept that he is God and he is the sacrifice for our sins. He is the cross we ought to cling to, for where he hung we now to get hang in freedom. Embodying his words and behavior will be like soaking in an insecticide that no worm ever dares nibble on.

When God gave us His Son and His Spirit he gave us access to **His power**. God is the most powerful being to ever exist. He created everything we see. He holds it all in his hand. He is that big. When he spoke the stars rode out to the galaxy on his breath. He sneezes and a hurricane happens. He coughs and it thunders. His finger is the tornado drawing scribbles upon the earth. I'm making some of this up, but it is a cool way to think of it, no? He has complete control and maximum authority. If we want a worm to flee, don't you think he can move it with less than a snap of his fingers? Please. Demons shiver in their boots at the mere mention of him. So why, I beg you, do we think our sin is too much for

God? Spray yourself. Remember his might. Acknowledge his authority. If so, worms won't stand a chance.

Since we are likely to minimize God's power, deny him full access to our hearts, and fail miserably at miming him, we were given others who are striving to do such things. God has established **the Church**. He knows there is power in accountability. We are resources to one another. People in your church are like muscles to you when you are weak. They are an insecticide when you are lacking to read the Bible on your own, see Jesus in the text, feel the Spirit in the quiet, or remember God's power working all around you. It is in the church that all these things should be visible. We should hear the Word. We should see Christ-like behavior. We should feel the Holy Spirit worship and be free. We should see God's powerful hand working - healing, giving, casting out demons, interpreting. When we are in the Church we should feel surrounded by God's company, empowered, uplifted, corrected, instructed, sprayed with insecticide. When we leave the Body of Christ we should feel ready to fend off any worms that may come our way.

Are you utilizing the insecticide of God? Are you trying to fight worms on your own? Are you wondering why you can't seem to overcome a certain sin when you haven't read your Bible in months or been in church for years? Newsflash. There are gallons of insecticide mixed up and ready for spraying. Get to reading. Get to praying. Get to church. Get to a small group. Get quiet and in the presence of God. Get back to realizing he has control and power and you don't. Get in his orchard. I implore you to go to His garden.

C. Austin Miles wrote a hymn about what it would be like to be "*In the Garden*." He said,

I come to the garden alone,
While the dew is still on the roses;
And the voice I hear, falling on my ear,
The Son of God discloses.
And He walks with me, and He talks with me,
And He tells me I am His own,
And the joy we share as we tarry there,
None other has ever known.

No greater space will ever be felt than to be in his presence. No greater place will ever exist than in his care. No greater path to be walked than where he has trod. Will you go there and stay? He certainly welcomes you.

Hi, my name is Kamra and I am so happy I just gotta tell you a little bit about the best Farmer I have ever known. My God has taken such good care of me. He's pruned a lot of things out of my life. Some of them were painful at the time, but it has all been for the better. He's shaping me and pruning me so I may produce the best kind of fruit. There's no place I'd rather be than in his presence. I'm one of God's happy little apples. Are you?

Chapter 9 Reflection

1. What are some differences between living in the wild versus God's Orchard?

2. Explain how God may prune something out of our lives. Give personal examples if you have any.

3. How did the fall in Genesis 3 change our garden circumstances?

God wants to spend time with you.

Label the illustration.

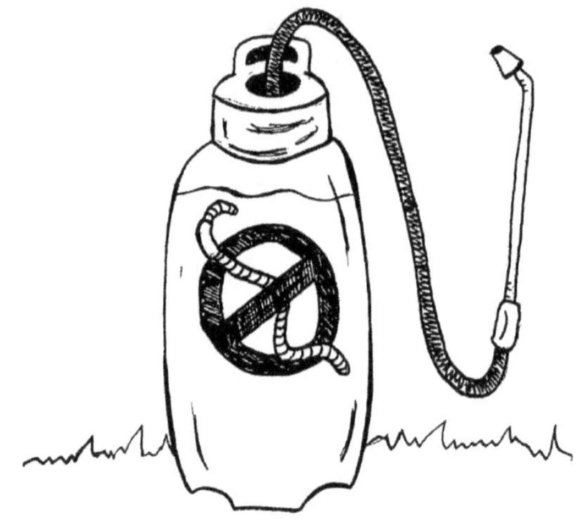

What are the five insecticides God has given us?

Chapter 9 Challenge

Choose one (Or all three if you're a go-getter!) to complete:

1) Pick one of the five insecticides below to soak in for thirty minutes.
•His Word: Read the Bible. (I recommend John 15)
•His Spirit: Sit in the quiet with no distractions (no screens or people) and pray / listen for God.
•His Son: Read in the Gospels. (Matthew, Mark, Luke or John)
•His Power: Find a place where you are reminded of God's power and sit in awe of him. While there, pray, listen, journal. OR, read about his powerful work in the Bible.
•His Body: Fellowship with like-minded believers from your Church, a small group, or in your community by praying together, listening to worship music or reading the Bible.

2) Camden suggested Adam and Eve cut down the tree God told them not to eat from. Is there something, or things, in your life that you know shouldn't be? List them, then be proactive in removing them. Ask God, the Great Farmer, to help. In addition, ask a trusted friend, pastor, or mentor to help you as well.

3) Do you know someone that is living in a wild patch? Will you share that good news with them?

If you are doing this study with a small group, make time to discuss this challenge with them and encourage one another.

Chapter 10
Grafted Back In

Now that we've reached the end of the book some of you may have read along and come to a thought similar to this: "What do I do now? I'm worm infested, have soft spots and bruises. My core is mushy, my stem is hanging on by a thread and I'm in a soil that isn't helping me grow one bit." Maybe it is only one of these dilemmas. Whatever it may be, I want to end this book by answering that question for you.

The answer is one of good news. I have the pleasure to assure you that you are not too far gone. You are not unseen. You are not alone. There is hope on the horizon. The Good Farmer is near.

"But, Kamra . . ." you may begin to protest. "You have no idea the condition I'm in. I'm rotting. I have worms inside me that are miles upon miles long. I have soft spots that have taken my core from bitter to downright hateful. My bruises are so big I could pass for a blue Smurf. There's no repairing this. I'm a lost cause."

I hear you and I once would have said the same about myself. The hospital visit that I mentioned in a previous chapter where I was put under suicide watch was no exaggeration. I truly wanted to end my life at one point. I felt hopeless and completely wrecked. I know what you may be feeling. I understand what you might be saying. It seems impossible to be healed. BUT we don't believe in a God of impossibilities, we believe in a God who makes all things possible.

When the apostle Paul was going through imprisonment and hardship we can only dare to imagine, he gave this quote to the Philippians (4:12-13):

I have experienced times of need and times of abundance. In any and every circumstance I have learned the secret of contentment, whether I go satisfied or hungry, have plenty or nothing. I am able to do all things through Christ who gives me strength.

Paul learned that there was no place too far from God's reach. There is nothing outside of God's realm. He can use our mistakes and troubles for His plans and purposes. Paul believed without a shadow of a doubt that because of Christ, he had the ability to push through.

If you believe in Jesus you ought to believe there isn't any state you can be in that he can't redeem, touch and bless. His strength is inside of his followers. That strength can bring them through the darkest times, the most brutal sin and the worst pain.

Do you believe Jesus is in you? If so, have faith that you can be cured from worms, your soft spots and bruises be healed, your stem and core strengthened, your skin armored, and your apple-status of a child of God be established. In all things. No matter where you find yourself today. You can be a clean, well-rounded, apple of the Good Farmer.

Getting healthy is not something you achieve on your own. Note in Paul's prior comment that his success was not due to his own strength - it was through Christ's. To get healthy and worm-free once more you don't have a step by step process to complete or so many good deeds to achieve. You don't have to be extra religious or super spiritual. There is only one thing to do: Believe in Jesus.

Faith is all it takes.

At the rise of the Christian church many Jews were having a hard time believing Gentiles could be in the family of God if they hadn't been circumcised and did certain things their Law required. It would become a whole debacle between apostles. It is talked about in nearly every New Testament book. The Jews were really fixated on the outward appearance, the rule-following. They were still trying to save themselves through good works, rituals and religion.

Paul was on the frontlines of combating this way of thinking. He even stood his ground against the disciple Peter on the matter. In the book of Romans he takes time to address the issue by illustration of tree grafting.

As mentioned in the seeds chapter, grafting is a way to establish what fruit will be produced from a tree. To graft you begin with a rootstock. This is the rooted section of the tree. It will be the base. It will control how tall the tree gets. Next, you cut a section from a fruit tree; that will be called the scion. This will be what produces the fruit you intend to eat.

After the scion is clipped, it is grafted into the rootstock. They each are cut and the scion is put into the rootstock. To hold them in place they are bound with grafting tape. Eventually, they will grow together to form one tree. Today, many of the fruit trees you purchase are from one piece of an original fruit tree being cut and grafted.

Paul uses this illustration of grafting to explain how God's people are like scions that can be grafted into his rootstock anytime. (Read Romans 11:17-24) Doing so will keep them from bearing a wild fruit. With him, the fruit they were meant to produce will be the most beautiful, tastiest and bountiful.

The Jews seem aggravated that Paul was preaching Gentiles could be grafted into the Tree of God. They thought it was their lineage, their rule-following and circumcised flesh that made them eligible to be a branch in God's tree. Paul corrects the matter by telling them it is only through faith in Jesus that one remains in God's tree. Indeed, if any one of them elected not to believe in Jesus they were broken off so others could be grafted in.

Broken off. Remember that pruning bit we talked about? This is it. When someone dies in their faith they become a dead branch that must be cut off. If a dead branch remains it will take up space where a new branch could shoot. Dead things have to be cut away so new life can flourish. God doesn't keep faithless branches. They are useless. Fruitless.

If you have lost all faith in Jesus, I warn you just as Paul warned the Roman readers: You will be cut off. When John the Baptist was calling people to put their faith in Jesus he declared:

"An ax is laid at the root of the trees,
and every tree that does not produce good fruit
will be cut down and thrown into the fire."
Matthew 3:10

Separation from God is death. Christ is the grafting tape that binds us with God. He made a way for us to be joined to God permanently. If we reject him, we reject the binding. We fall away. We become a stick. Dead branches are the kindling for hell's fire. Those who don't believe in Jesus are Satan's firewood.

If you have lost your faith in Jesus, you can be grafted back in. Paul said to take note of the kindness of God. "If you do not continue in your unbelief you will be grafted in, for God is able to graft them in again" (11:23). Again. He is a God of second chances. He is a God of forgiveness. He is a God who longs for all of his creation to be with him. He doesn't want a single one of us to perish. He'd rather Hell be frozen over, not a flame in sight. If you want back in, he is overjoyed to graft you back in. Again and again and again.

If you decidedly fell away from God and rolled into the wild, God is calling you back and he's doing so softly and tenderly. That is why Will L. Thompson wrote

Softly and tenderly Jesus is calling,
calling for you and for me;
see, on the portals he's waiting and watching,
watching for you and for me.
Come home, come home;
you who are weary come home;
earnestly, tenderly, Jesus is calling,
calling, O sinner, come home!
Why should we tarry when Jesus is pleading,
pleading for you and for me?
Why should we linger and heed not his mercies,
mercies for you and for me?
-"Softly and Tenderly Jesus is Calling"

There is nowhere too far that you could have rolled. There's no place too dark that God has not seen you hiding. His arms stretched upon the cross shows you just how far he's willing to reach and how painfully long he will hang to get your attention. So I tell you, roll on home little apples. Like the prodigal son your Dad is waiting to take you back under His good care (see Luke 15:11-32).

Declaring you do not have faith in Jesus is a clear way to be cut off from God's rootstock, but some people will never admit that. Instead they will fall away from the tree through a different means - they will rot off.

Perhaps you haven't denied that Jesus is Lord and God is Creator. Maybe your faith in Him isn't the issue. Maybe you are simply corrupt with sin, infested with worms. You know what is right and what is wrong but you have willingly let wrong override all that is right. You saw the worm coming and you let him in. You invited other worms to come to the feast too. You just plopped down in the tub of sin and took a bath. You let it all soak in and now you aren't sure if there's even a scrap of good skin, seeds and core left. You are rotting and wasting away.

I'll tell you this, you aren't going to be cut off but that is because you're going to fall away all on your own if you let yourself stay in that state. If you choose to remain in a swimming pool of sin then you are going to get so waterlogged, so much core damage, that your stem will disintegrate and you will fall away on your own accord.

God doesn't want you to rot away. He grafted you in because he had a beautiful purpose for you. But if you choose to sin you are electing to die. You are not choosing life. You are voting on President Shame, Governor Guilt, and the Diplomat of Death. Is that really what you want to rule your life? Open your eyes! That sinful path is rancid. What's more is God won't allow it. When an apple gets infested with worms it threatens all the surrounding apples' health. When a farmer finds a worm infestation, he cuts off the branch in order to keep the whole tree from becoming infected. Likewise, if you're a demon-obeying, sin-enslaved, worm-infested apple of a person, God won't let you stay in his tree. It threatens the well-being of his orchard and puts his own reputation as a good Farmer at risk. Can't happen. Won't happen.

If you're there, slowly decomposing because of sin, there is a rescue. Jesus was crucified upon a tree and rose from the dead in order that we may have access to the Tree of Life once more. Through his battle on Calvary we can know the war on sin has been won. We do not have to succumb to the sinful nature. We have been given access to the Spirit who fights against the sinful nature.

For the desires of the flesh are against the Spirit,
and the desires of the Spirit are against the flesh,
for these are opposed to each other,
to keep you from doing the things you want to do.
Galatians 5:17

The Spirit is here to help us fight against the sins that we want to commit. I know it can be hard to say no to unhealthy things sometimes. Our body can be powerful. Our hearts can fall so hard and our minds can be so twisted. But this is why we discussed in length how important having tough skin is and the amount of God. We have to be wrapped in the Spirit. We have to be obedient to Him. If we are, he can transform us from rot to spotless.

Therefore, if anyone is in Christ, the new creation has
come: The old has gone, the new is here!
2 Corinthians 5:17

Jesus can take a rotten, wormy apple and make it new. If he can die and rise from the dead, he can bring a decaying apple back to life. Your sin is not too much. Your worm isn't too big. If you try to do it all on your own, it's impossible. But with Him, nothing is impossible.

If you feel like you don't deserve a new start I want to stop you right there. That lie will keep you in death's grip. Satan has you right where he wants you if you think you aren't worthy to be made new. The price has already been paid. Christ can't be un-crucified. If you refuse to take him up on his ability to refresh your soul you are wasting a perfect sacrifice. You are saying his blood wasn't red enough, his beating not as bad as your bruising, his resurrection not all that miraculous. If you honestly think any of that then you need to watch *The Passion* movie. Just watch how Jesus was whipped with the cat of nine tails. See how he was stabbed and how a crown of thorns was jabbed into his skull. If you think you can't catch your breath, imagine the suffocating pressure he went through while hanging from his palms on the cross, while his lungs filled with blood and water, and his legs became too weak to push up his chest for air.

If you believe that much of your sin, that you're unsavable, then you don't believe enough in my Savior.

None of us are perfect. We all sin (1 John 1:8). We all will fall short of the glory of God (Romans 3:23). We all will stink up the earth every now and then with our rotten behavior. But guess what, we don't have to live in that identity, in that lifestyle. We can say no to sin and say, "I am saved through Jesus. Not saved by myself. It is a gift from God" (Ephesians 2:8). Your life can turn around because we have a conjunction kind of God. We have a "but" God.

A conjoining word is one that connects two phrases. It brings one thing into a new light. It can complete a meaning. Some conjoining words are "and, if, so, yet, also... and but." Our God is the conjunction that takes us from death to life, from rotten to alive.

"We formerly lived out our lives in the cravings of our flesh, indulging in the desires of the flesh and the mind, and were by nature children of wrath. But God, being rich in mercy, because of his great love with which he loved us, even though we were dead in our sin, made us alive together with Christ - for it is by grace we are saved." Ephesians 2:4-5

You were sinful, yes. You were rotten, I got you. BUT you don't have to be. You were made for much more. You, my friend, were made to be enjoyed and to enjoy God.

Your story is not over, though this particular one is concluding. I hope I've left you on an encouraging note. I hope you have been spurred on to be the best apple you can be by being as close as you can to the Good Farmer. If we all worked to achieve this, the world would be one beautiful garden, just as God intended it to be. In the meantime, we have to keep pressing forward. If we do, the reward will be worth it.

Then the angel showed me the river of the water of life,
as clear as crystal, flowing from the throne of God
and of the Lamb down the middle of the great street of
the city. On each side of the river stood the tree of life,
bearing twelve crops of fruit, yielding its fruit every
month. And the leaves of the tree are for the healing of
the nations. No longer will there be any curse.
The throne of God and of the Lamb will be in the city,
and his servants will serve him.
They will see his face, and his name will be on their
foreheads. There will be no more night.
They will not need the light of a lamp or the light of the
sun, for the Lord God will give them light.
And they will reign forever and ever.
Revelation 22:1-5

One day the Garden of Eden will be restored. God's beautiful apples will hang in heaven without a care in the world. All that we tried to practice so earnestly here will be easy to accomplish there. We will be with the Tree of Life. We won't die or rot or get soft spots or bruises. We won't need to cry and confess because there won't be sin. We will be without blemish. Our skin will be covered, flawless, perfected. We will be un-graft-able. It'll be permanent. Fixed. Worth it.

Can you hold on until then?

Chapter 10 Reflection

1. What does one have to do to be grafted into God's Tree?

2. There are a variety of reasons a person may be separated from God. This chapter mentions "being a dead branch, rolling away, and rotting." What has separated you from God?

3. What will the life for a believer look like in Heaven, as mentioned in Revelation 22?

When you are grafted into God's Tree, you become one with Him. He never wishes to part from you.

Label the illustration.

Who is the Rootstock, the Scion, the binding tape & the Farmer?

Chapter 10 Challenge

Choose one (Or all three if you're still yearning for more!) to complete:

1) Share your testimony.
With someone you haven't shared with before, make time to tell them how you were grafted into God's Tree. If you have not accepted Jesus as your grafting tape, talk with someone about how to become a part of the family of God. Ask questions and seek wise counsel.

2) Share the Good News.
 If you have accepted Jesus as your grafting tape and are part of the Tree of God, share the story of Jesus with someone. Read Scripture with them, pray and have honest conversation about where they are (in God's Orchard, rolled away, rotting, etc.). You do not have to get them to accept Jesus or say a "sinner's prayer". You need only share the message found in the Word through the Spirit.

3) Share thanks.
Think of key people in your life who have shown you Jesus and helped you get to, or remain in, God's Orchard.
- First, personally thank them for their influence, their words and prayers by sharing your words of thanks. Write them a note, email, text or call them, or have a chat face to face over coffee or dinner.
- Second, thank them through a gift. This can be paying for their coffee or meal, giving them a token, a card, a picture, etc. Be creative and be genuine.

Next, thank God.

- First, in a sincere verbal prayer, or handwritten / typed note, tell God thanks for what he has done in your life - his tending, pruning, sending his Son to mend you together, grafting you back in, etc.
- Second, give God a gift. I know that can sound crazy, but obviously this isn't going to be a literal hand-to-hand gift-giving. But there are plenty of ways you can show God how you appreciate what He has done in your life in a special way. Here's some ideas: a tithe of money, an offering of finances to a person who is laid on your heart, singing him a song, writing him a poem, painting or drawing him something, taking a meal to a neighbor, etc. Remember, everything you do for others, you do for him as well. Whatever you choose to do, have it in mind that it is a special gift for God.

If you are doing this study with a small group, make time to discuss this challenge with them and encourage one another.